ROCKSTAR RISING

ROCKSTAR RISING

How to Turn Resilience Into Your Superpower

Adrianne Fekete

©2025 All Rights Reserved. No portion of this book may be reproduced, stored in a retrieval system, or transmitted in any form or by any means—electronic, mechanical, photocopy, recording, scanning, or other—except for brief quotations in critical reviews or articles without the prior permission of the author.

Published by Game Changer Publishing

Paperback ISBN: 978-1-968250-42-3

Hardcover ISBN: 978-1-968250-43-0

Digital ISBN: 978-1-968250-44-7

www.GameChangerPublishing.com

*To my Four Legends — Noah, Nico, Hunter, and Mateo — thank you
for growing with me, believing in me, and clapping when the world was quiet.
You are the heartbeat behind my hustle, and your love made me brave.
You are my greatest adventure and my proudest reason why.
Thank you for being the kind of men who cheer for strong women.
You are my greatest success story.*

*To my Father — my hero, who showed me how to lead with heart
and never doubt my worth. Your strength lit my path, and your voice
still reminds me I can do anything. Thank you
for always seeing the warrior in me.*

*To my Mother — your love is the backbone of every brave thing I've done.
Your strength, your sass, and your love built the woman I became.
You are my forever fan, whose love is stitched into every word I write.
Your love has never wavered. Not once. Thank you
for loving me fiercely through every chapter.*

*To my Husband — thank you for letting me dream loud, love big,
and rise unapologetically. Thank you for never flinching when I set the world
on fire chasing my dreams. You've stood beside the storm and still chose
to dance in the rain with me. This book is inked in our legacy.*

READ THIS FIRST

Welcome to Your Rise; This Is the Beginning of Everything

The struggle is part of the story. And so is your comeback. Whether you whispered "enough" or screamed "I'm ready," something brought you here—and that something matters.

Rockstar Rising is more than a collection of chapters. It's a mirror, a mission, and a movement. It's proof that your past doesn't define you—your decision to rise does.

Your Comeback Starts Here!

I created a space where bold women rise and legends are made. But it is not just a brand—it's a global movement for those who lead, build, and break the mold.

But rising isn't meant to be done alone. That's why I built the I Am Unbreakable® with our Front Row Sisterhood community in the forefront—a place where the boldest, fiercest, most resilient women gather to support, strategize, and soar. Not someday—now.

This is the moment everything changes.
The front row is waiting for you.

No More Sidelines. No More Silence. Just You, Rising.

Scan the QR code to step into the room built for women who are done waiting. You're not behind. You're right on time.

**YOU DIDN'T JUST PICK UP A BOOK.
YOU ANSWERED A CALL.**

Scan the QR Code Here:

ROCKSTAR RISING
HOW TO TURN RESILIENCE INTO YOUR SUPERPOWER

ADRIANNE FEKETE

AUTHOR'S NOTE

This book wasn't written in a quiet corner. It was written in the chaos—in the moments I wanted to quit, when the world said "too much," and I decided to be even bolder.

This isn't a success story.

It's a survival story. A rise story.

A reminder that resilience is built in the messy middle.

And it's about the courage to rewrite your story when the old one no longer fits.

I've been underestimated. Counted out.

Told to stay small, stay silent, stay nice.

But I chose to bet on myself—every time.

AUTHOR'S NOTE

And through it all, I've discovered that confidence isn't born—it's built. Unapologetically. One bold decision at a time.

You don't need to earn your worth. You already have it.

You don't need to be perfect. You need to be powerful.

You don't need to become more.

You need to remember who you are.

You don't need to wait for your moment.

This is the moment.

You'll learn to lead yourself through the chaos—not in spite of it, but because of it—owning every scar as part of your comeback.

I wrote this for the one who shows up, even when her confidence doesn't.

For the woman who's still figuring it out.

The one who's still fighting to believe in herself.

For the woman who's strong, but exhausted.

For the one who knows deep down—there's more —and is ready to go get it.

So here it is—my story, my scars, my rise.

Not for applause.

AUTHOR'S NOTE

But to remind you: YOUR rise is already in motion.

And it starts right here.

Let's go.

Adrienne
xoxo

CONTENTS

Introduction	xv
1. Rockstar Confidence	1
2. The Resilience Revolution	9
3. Rejection is Redirection	23
4. Manifest Like A Rockstar	31
5. The Three F-Bombs	41
6. Own Your Shift	51
7. Nice Gut	61
8. Comfortable Being Uncomfortable	69
9. Perfectly Imperfect	77
10. From Trauma to Purpose	87
11. The Power of I Am	101
12. You Are a Rockstar	107
Conclusion	115
Bonus Chapters	121
13. Your Personal Private Investigator	123
14. Red Flag Moments	125
15. Hot P.I. Topics	139
Thank You for Rising With Us	181

INTRODUCTION

"I never wanted to be the girl who played it safe. I wanted to be the girl who took risks and believed in herself."
~ Joan Jett

Your struggle wasn't a detour. It's the training ground. I've walked through chaos. I've experienced failures. I lived through the loss and trauma. I've sat in the silence after everything fell apart. I've rebuilt from the ruins more times than I can count. And through it all, one truth kept rising: *You don't need permission to rise. You already are the comeback.* This book wasn't written from a pedestal—it was written from the trenches. From the raw, unfiltered, battle-tested truth of what it takes to believe in yourself when nobody else does. When the lights are off. When your name's not called. When the dream feels heavy, and the doubt feels louder than the fire in your gut. But you didn't quit. You didn't crumble. You kept showing up. Even bruised. Even breathless. And that is **Rockstar Confidence™**.

It's not a mood. It's a mission. It's the decision to stand tall in a world that benefits when you play small. It's the energy that says, *I know who I am. I know why I'm here. And I will not be silenced.* Confidence

INTRODUCTION

isn't handed to you. It's built. Built in heartbreak. Built in rejection. Built in every moment you whispered, "I've got me," when no one else did. I'm not here to hand you motivation. I'm here to remind you of what you already know deep down: You're a damn force. You've already survived what was meant to destroy you. You've already risen after what tried to bury you. You've already shown the world that your power can't be stolen, bought, or faked. This is your edge. Your superpower.

As an award-winning media expert for the Rolling Stones and U2, 8X founder, and North America's first female private investigator agency owner, I've spent my life walking into rooms I wasn't invited to —and building empires on the other side.

Now, I help others do the same through **I Am Unbreakable**®, a visibility engine—a multimedia platform for trailblazing women who lead, disrupt, and rise.

I connect women-led businesses with strategic partners, media leaders, and elite investors who help them scale and create impact and influence. My mission is to amplify opportunity, funding, and the remarkable voices that drive social impact, create legacies, and foster belonging.

I am the Canadian Ambassador for the Women Presidents Organization, an Advisory Council Member for Women Funding Women and Women Get On Board, and a member of various mission-driven boards.

I ignite change by sharing unfiltered stories through keynotes, videos, live experiential events, and editorial content. When I am not interviewing on the highly rated *I Am Unbreakable*® Podcast, which is available on YouTube, Spotify, Apple, and Amazon Podcast, you will find me on a stage speaking about relevant business strategies and hot self-improvement topics.

Connection, belonging, community, collaboration, and social impact are at the heart of my leadership approach.

Other interesting facts are that I am a mental health advocate, a

INTRODUCTION

mother of four incredible boys, and the proud owner of a junior hockey team in the world's largest league. My mission? To drive legacy, leadership, and lasting impact. **Because the struggle isn't a detour—it's the training ground.**

They told me I wasn't smart enough. That my grades weren't good enough. That I didn't have the intellect, or the money, or the drive to be anything. I refused to let someone else define what I could become. Their words were not my truth. In life, you're the writer, director, editor, narrator, and lead actor. You can flip the script anytime you choose. Your belief, your drive, and your work ethic will determine who you become.

If I had to describe myself in five words? **Leather. Lipstick. Rock 'n' roll. Pink. Bling**. But if I'm being real: *authentic, resilient, passionate, purposeful, and kind*. I'm the woman in the gym, kickboxing through a back and neck injury. I'm the mom of four boys, cheering in the hockey stands with fierce dedication. I'm the daughter, sister, wife, and friend known for my huge heart, kind spirit, big hair, resilient mindset, and never backing down when I believe in something or somebody.

At ten years old, I caught the entrepreneurial bug. I knew it was my calling. At seventeen I was told I was not smart enough and that I would amount to nothing. At nineteen, I opened my first business and sold it five years later at a profit. At twenty-four, I launched a public relations agency and worked with clients like the Rolling Stones, U2, Samuel L. Jackson, and the WWE. That's where Rockstar Confidence was born. Working with legends taught me about failure, grit, and staying grounded under pressure.

At thirty, I became the first female founder in North America to own a fully licensed private investigations and security agency. Imagine living as a trauma expert, hostage negotiator, therapist, emergency operator, and WWE referee all in one. That was my life for decades. When people think of private investigators, they imagine a man in a trench coat and black fedora, lurking in the shadows. That was very yesterday. I built my business on truth, empathy, and tenacity.

INTRODUCTION

In the early years, I faced online threats, stalking, even cinder blocks thrown through my windows—just for being a woman in a male-dominated industry. But I stayed true to myself. Because I knew: The struggle is part of the story. It's the chapter where growth happens.

Folks refer to me as a modern-day Nancy Drew because I built an award-winning private investigation agency from the ground up. I know, you want to hear a story, right? Everyone loves a good PI story.

No two days are the same. Just when I think I've heard the most "out there" story, another real-life situation requires investigation.

Private investigation is one of the most emotionally charged careers. That's where I come in with my Louis Vuitton purse, blond hair flying, and ready to slay the day. I'll have my shoulders back and my chin up with twenty solutions for every problem my clients throw at me.

Each day is "out there." Some are just more challenging and rarer than others, and most are totally unforgettable from the moment my phone rings and someone says, "I need your help."

Take the case I'll call *"Family Feud Meets Wedding Bell Hell."*

The story begins on an average Thursday night when my phone rings. The voice on the other end is male. He cuts right to the chase.

"I'm Mark, and I'm getting married Saturday night. And I need evidence that my fiancée is screwing around."

Hello! My response: "You couldn't have called me Wednesday?" I said in a soft voice, and even he chuckled.

Forty-eight hours wasn't much time to change his entire future—or not, but I've always liked a challenge.

This story revolved around the caller Mark and the lovely Melissa, who looked like a dream couple from a magazine ad. Both were from very prominent families, with hers being off-the-charts successful and regular bold faces in the gossip columns for their charitable works. He was thirty-eight, handsome, fit, with black slicked-back hair and a booming business. She was a few years younger, a beautiful, petite girl with a warm, sunny smile.

They were the perfect couple, which doesn't exist.

INTRODUCTION

Oh, hell to the no.

In my unpredictable world, nothing is as it seems. No one is entirely trusted... until I check them out.

I'll say it a thousand times to anyone who will listen: *PI tip—knowledge is power.*

The toughest part of my job is vetting each and every person's intention of why they want to investigate whatever they're calling me about in the first place. Are their intentions truthful? Are they solid individuals? Are there any mental health issues? Do they have a criminal record or intention? This is the most important part of the process.

No, I won't run over your deadbeat, cheating, lying wife or husband with my car. We don't shake people down for money they owe you. Nor do we run a hit squad.

My entire team consists of former police sergeants, executives, and specialty unit detectives. We're your modern-day A-Team (lol!).

The above-mentioned Mark was getting hitched in forty-eight hours. Let's take a bit of a deeper look. He also had a feeling that his dream woman was doing the nasty thing with another guy, and Mark was remarkably level-headed. I took the case and put one of my investigators on it and also complied with a strange request. Mark asked if a few members of my PI firm could attend the actual wedding. Yes, he was going through with the nuptials, no matter what we found out, which was a bit odd.

"All I can tell you is it won't go over well," Mark promised with a delicious laugh.

Great news. Just wonderful.

Cut to twenty-four hours before the big day. You didn't have to have a background in private investigations to catch Melissa, the hot pants bride who wasn't exactly doing dress fittings and trying out new hairdos in the hours leading up to the big day.

"Mark, I'm so sorry," I had to inform him. "She's not only screwing different guys in the backseat of her car... we have it on video." It's always hard to tell clients thing like this but his fiancée was moaning

INTRODUCTION

and groaning in several naked ass shots. I'm talking heads bobbing up and down and feet in the air.

"But, there's more. Yesterday, she was legs up in the car, butt naked, doing the horizontal mambo with your best man, Tim," he said.

I waited for the explosion. The tears. The raging.

"You will be at the wedding because I'll be at the wedding," Mark repeated.

"What are you going to do?" I asked again. I wanted to brief my guys who had been hired for executive protection.

"Trust me," he said.

Cut to the big day. The sky was blue, the birds were chirping, and the groom was about to go off the rails.

CUT!!! You didn't think I was going to give away the end here, did you? You will find the details, lessons, and humor soon—TRUST ME!

One of my favorite sayings is, "The struggle is part of the story." So many of us want to believe in the fairy tales of life, but the universe has a unique way of revealing our true path. I know that funny feeling when something feels very wrong, and I trust it.

One of my mentors, Oprah, says, "When I don't listen to my instincts, is when I get myself in trouble."

People who *do* listen to that little inner voice of wisdom call me for help, which shouldn't be looked at as a shameful thing. I always tell people to listen to their bodies. You are listening to your heart and soul and reaching out for help, which is actually quite an empowering act. Many of my clients will say to me, "Adrianne, I just want to know the truth. Please find the truth."

Most people are searching for answers, reasons to take the next steps, and the "money shot" of somebody doing what their intuition is telling them is going on. I ask clients one thing: Trust the process. For people to trust me, I need to connect with them instantly. Sometimes, they give me thirty seconds or a minute. They need to know I understand them and will never judge them. Their innermost secrets are safe with me.

INTRODUCTION

I have worked alongside the most iconic musicians, celebrities, athletes, actors, and dignitaries to find their truth. That could be another book, but those secrets will die with me. The personal life of my clients is just that... personal. I'm the founder and president of Star Quality Private Investigations, a national award-winning agency named by many publications as Toronto's number one private investigation firm. Regardless of achievements and obstacles, my mantra has never changed: I always wanted to do the best and be the best for my clients. I believe in people stepping into their own power regardless of gender. I've been told I'm not someone who will back down easily.

I listen to Mötley Crüe before breakfast, answer clients' calls all day long, and grab my green juice after I do my hair and lipstick.

A born entrepreneur with a "girls can do anything" mentality, the word "can't" doesn't exist unless I'm going for the third piece of chocolate. (Then I definitely say, "No, sorry, I can't.") I go into everything with a rock star attitude. What does that mean? That means no matter what I do, when or where I do it, I give one thousand percent. My moral compass is never compromised, with integrity and trust at the forefront. I may not succeed each time, but when I lay my head down at night, I know I haven't crossed any lines in the sand.

But here's what matters most: I show up for people when their world is falling apart, and the most astonishing transformation happens. They come to me looking for the truth about someone else, and yet they leave with a deeper truth about themselves. It is profound.

This is where they learn to own their shift. And that means getting real. Looking in the mirror, like my rockstar friend Angela Bassett says, "When you look in the mirror, you better love what you see." If you don't love it yet, that's okay. You've got the power to change it. You just have to ask: *Do I stay in what's comfortable? Or do I lean into the shift and trust myself?*

Your struggle wasn't the setback—it was the setup for your rise.

You didn't pick up this book to be inspired. You picked it up because some part of you is *done waiting*. Done playing by rules you

INTRODUCTION

never agreed to. Done shrinking, hiding, second-guessing, and making yourself small just to make others comfortable. You picked this up because you're ready to rise. To own your story. To *build something legendary* from everything they thought would break you.

This isn't self-help. This is *self-leadership*. This is confidence without conditions. Power without permission. Clarity without apology. You don't need a map—you *are* the blueprint. You don't need more credentials—you need to trust your own fire. And if the world hasn't made space for your voice yet? Good. You're here to *build your own stage*. This book will challenge you, shake you, and call you up—but only if you let it.

So here's the truth:

You're not here to be chosen. You're here to choose yourself.

You're not here to chase confidence. You're here to own it.

You're not here to blend in. You're here to lead out loud.

You're not waiting to become the Rockstar.

You already are.

Let's rise.

CHAPTER ONE
ROCKSTAR CONFIDENCE

*"You've always had the power, my dear.
You just had to learn it for yourself."*
~ Glinda, Wizard of Oz

Rockstar Confidence isn't just a mindset—it's a *movement*. It's the fierce, unshakable energy that pulses through trailblazing women who are building empires, breaking rules, and redefining leadership on their own terms. It's not about being the loudest in the room. It's about owning the damn room the moment you walk in.

It's about showing up boldly in boardrooms, meetings, summits, and on stages with a voice that doesn't ask for permission but commands attention. Rockstar Confidence is what fuels female founders who go first. The disruptors who build what's never been built. The women who launch brands from scratch, raise capital like legends, and pitch ideas that shake industries. These are the women who don't shrink to fit in—they expand to lead. They don't just play the game—they rewrite the rules. They don't just talk about impact—they become the impact.

This confidence doesn't come from waiting to be chosen. It's forged in fire. It's built through failure, discipline, audacity, and showing up every single day, even when the world tells you to sit down. Rockstar Confidence is the ultimate power source behind change-making women. It's your edge. Your fire. Your revolution. If you're a builder, a founder, or a visionary who's ready to stop playing small and start leading like a legend…

You're not just confident. You're *Rockstar* Confident.

As the founder of a fairly successful public relations and event company, for Mick Jagger's sixtieth birthday, I was responsible for ensuring the entire crew got the fifty-thousand-square-foot mansion we had rented ready for the festivities. I searched for the perfect plates and cutlery, pristine white with a gold rim, and watched the caterers bring in the food. A whirlwind of provisions moved around me. I felt like I was directing traffic. Or, at the very least, just trying to stay out of the way.

The event and my relationship with the Rolling Stones meant a lot to me. I had worked hard to get there, to that exact place, to that exact time in my life. I felt like I was on the precipice of something beautiful, something better than the life I had been living. But while I had ambition and was running my own successful business, I hadn't yet recognized all of my gifts, nor had I learned all I needed to know. I still felt unsettled—probably because I had spent many of the previous few years as a single mother, living with my own mother for the support that she had so generously offered me.

A few days before Jagger's birthday, I found out that I had been invited to a rehearsal. The Stones had rented out a nearby middle school for their auditorium and practice rooms, as well as a hangar at Pearson. For several months, they had been working out the acoustics on their new album all over Toronto, and it was finally time to bring everyone together. That night, I settled into the room with the crew, the band's family members, and their friends. I felt special. I looked up as Jagger's voice cut across the room. He had stepped up to the mic, singing "Angie." I was mesmerized, drawn into the lyrics and the sound. *Was he singing to me?* I thought. *He meant Adrianne, not Angie, right?*

The song is about love, of course, about a couple who are on the verge of losing each other. They have nothing, no money, and they're at the precipice of despair. But when Jagger sings, it's clear there is still love between them. There is still hope. Lost in the music, I thought of my journey from hope to despair to hope again. My life, like that of so many other people, has been marked by moments, days, and sometimes, years of trauma. I was strong, but I wasn't "perfectly" strong. I knew what Jagger meant. I knew that sense of "almost" lost hope and what it meant to start to believe again.

To me, Jagger sounded perfect. As the song ended, he struck the first chord of "Angie" for a second time, and then a third, and I couldn't walk away—I just stayed and listened, trying to catch his eye. With each run-through, each version of the song was slightly different, slightly more perfect. He repeated the words again and again until he got it right for himself, not for me or anyone else in earshot. He wanted to get the song right for himself, and every time he sang the chorus, he smiled. Repeating every note felt good to him. He didn't waver or seem bored, angry, or tired. He just smiled. Listening to Jagger, my understanding of what it took to become whole shifted. I knew then what it truly meant to have Rockstar Confidence: to make yourself a promise and keep it, no matter what.

Your confidence doesn't need to be perfect—it needs to be practiced. This mantra is something I have lived by, something I teach all my clients and anybody who will listen. The neat thing about Rockstar Confidence is you pick it, you get to change it, you get to shift it. Because as we all know, life's a journey, not a destination. We are all very fluid, and we're all works in progress.

Life isn't about being perfect; it's about confidence. It's the standard you hold yourself to. To me, Rockstar Confidence is the promise you make to yourself and keep when no one else is looking. Being confident is about cultivating your superpower potential. It's giving yourself the permission to be the person you want to be, authentically, without hesitation. Being confident means having trust in yourself, knowing that you will be able to navigate all the obstacles that life sets out before you. Being confident is about bending like a tree in a storm, rather than collapsing under the weight of the world, when things go wrong. Being confident means becoming wholly and fully you. And the first step in becoming authentically you is developing the kind of Rockstar Confidence that I observed in Mick Jagger.

Confidence isn't external. It's a standard you live by. At the end of the day, Rockstar Confidence is about making a promise to yourself, keeping it, and not veering from that. Remember, if you would like to change what that means to you, that is a decision you make alone. When I am looking into the eyes of an obstacle, I check in with myself to make sure I am doing the best I can do to navigate it, to live through it with grace, and to understand the gold on the other side, which is growth.

As long as you can lay your head down at night and say, *You know what? I did the best I could do.* Knowing that you did the "best I could do" today, whatever that looks like in the moment, is where the magic lives.

To me, becoming unbreakable means getting up, moving forward, and getting through whatever life throws our way. It means rising when you don't want to, when life tries to hold you down, and you have nothing left in the tank; you get up and do it anyway. You show up for yourself because it is you who has to come stand up and move forward. Snail's pace or 100 miles per hour, movement is movement. You stand up, show up, and move forward, no matter what! No matter how hard. No matter how many times. Show up authentically, be vulnerable, and believe that no matter what the outcome, you are going to be okay.

When private investigative clients first retain our services, they often come wearing several suits of armor, or, as it is often referred to, a mask. If you are wearing a suit of armor that no longer serves you, it is blocking your growth. If you can't be your authentic self, then you're living the life of somebody else. It will never fit properly, and you will never succeed at whatever you're trying to do personally or professionally.

Working alongside some of the most incredible legends taught me so much about failure, grit, perseverance, and resilience. It was a *Yes, You Can* all day long.

When I look back at where I came from, I believe that I always innately had self-belief inside of me. But there was a block. It was something I personally needed to believe in. I needed to choose, and yes, it was that simple. I didn't say the path was easy; I said the choice to believe in yourself is simple. My life immediately shifted. I realized that confidence isn't something you wait to feel—it's something you earn when you show up bleeding and still say, "Let's go!"

We are not here to fit in—we are here to stand out. We are not waiting to be chosen—we are choosing *ourselves*. We are women, humans, founders, trailblazers, visionaries, and disruptors. We build from nothing. We lead with fire. We draw strength from near nothing, and then we rise like legends.

This confidence doesn't come from waiting to be chosen.

It's forged in fire.

It's built through failure, discipline, audacity, and showing up every single day—even when the world tells you to sit down.

Rockstar Confidence is the ultimate power source behind change-making women.

Our confidence and resilience aren't conditional. They're not quiet. They're not polite. They're bold, relentless, and unapologetic. We wear failure like battle scars. We don't fear the fall—we own the comeback. When they say we're *too much*, we say, "Good. More is coming."

Rockstar Confidence is a promise we make to ourselves every single day:

To show up.

To speak up.

To shake things up.

We don't play small.

We play BOLD.

Your belief becomes your boldness. Your presence becomes your power. And your love becomes your legacy.

This is Rockstar Confidence.

And it's your *edge*. Your *fuel*. Your *fire*.

ROCKSTAR RECAP

Confidence is not something you wait to feel—it's something you decide to own by living up to the promise you make yourself. It begins behind closed doors, in private, when no one is clapping or cheering you on.

NOTE: At the end of this book, you will find my **Rockstar Confidence Action Checklist** to track your growth by reflecting on each chapter's key action step.

Journal Prompts For Readers

★ When was the last time you held yourself to a higher standard even though no one witnessed it?

_____
_____
_____
_____

★ What's a suit of armor you've worn that you're now ready to drop?

_____
_____
_____
_____

★ How does it feel to choose confidence before others see it in you?

_____
_____
_____
_____

Make Your Move
Record a voice memo of three affirmations that reflect who you are when you're most authentic. Play it to yourself every morning.

CHAPTER TWO
THE RESILIENCE REVOLUTION

"Rock bottom became the solid foundation on which I rebuilt my life."
~ J.K. Rollins

Resilience isn't just about bouncing back—it's about rising on purpose. It's the quiet choice to keep going when no one's clapping. It's showing up with a steady fire when everything around you is shaking.

I used to think resilience was something you found *after* everything fell apart, but I learned early in life that it lives inside you *before* the fall. Resilience is forged in the unglamorous moments—the rejection, the redirection, the rebuild. It's not about how fast you bounce back, but about how deeply you root in your purpose when nothing makes sense. You don't have to wait for the dust to settle to remember who you are. You lean in and go through it. You build in the middle of it.

This isn't about being unaffected. It's about being unstoppable. When life tries to dim you, resilience says, "Watch me shine anyway."

When it gets hard, resilience kicks in—not with noise, but with certainty. The world tells you to be realistic. Resilience tells you to be relentless. This isn't about bouncing. This is about becoming. And that? That's the revolution.

I'd like to share a few stories about my mother, Catherine (a.k.a. Mamazita), Hungarian Mama, Grandma, Laundry Commander, Nerf Gunner Extraordinaire, and Queen of Everything. All joking aside, she is my rock.

She is eighty-nine years young—smart, driven, well-read, strong, funny, dedicated, and loving. My father, Laszlo, was the tougher of the two. He pushed me to become the person I am today. While other girls were sewing and baking with their moms, I was building fences and putting up drywall with my dad.

We did a lot of "boy" things together because he wanted me to be independent and to know how to do everything. Gender was irrelevant in our house. My friends could bake cookies, but I could construct a treehouse. We loved spending time together doing those kinds of things—something I would later recognize as one of my earliest experiences of being a girl doing things typically associated with men.

I feel incredibly lucky to have had both of them as my parents, as they set me on my path. Being an entrepreneur and a mother was always the fuel that set my heart on fire. My parents were my example. No one worked harder. No one had a better work ethic. No one survived the way that they did. They created a life together regardless of obstacles.

Back to my mother for a moment. As a little girl, she would tell me the stories of her days as a young girl growing up in Hungary in a small city that imploded during the Hungarian Revolution. Life changed when the Russians came to Europe, and Hungary got pulled into a Communist regime. Mom remembers the horrifying day when, as a little seven-year-old girl, she opened her front door and a military man was towering above her, holding a machine gun to her face. Her father, Regga, who at the time owned a very successful heating and electrical company in Hungary and Austria, was taken into military custody.

"I was crying and crying," my mother recalls of that day when everything changed. "The Russians took my daddy away. We didn't know if we would ever see him again or if they would kill him. I also thought they might find out that my mother was Jewish and had recently converted to Roman Catholic."

Miracles did happen. Her father came home hours later and refused to talk about what happened to him that day. My grandfather told his little girl, my mother, that the only important thing was that he survived, and he would make sure that the family would stay together. "We didn't go anywhere. They allowed us to stay in our own house," Mom told me. "It didn't seem fair because it was our house. They claimed it to be their house now and took all of our valuables, collectibles, money, and anything that wasn't nailed to the ground. My father said, 'It's okay. At least we survived.'"

A family dedicated to public service, she watched her own mother and father take the little bit of money that wasn't taken from them and distribute some of it to the poor. This made it evident that your DNA footprint has such an impact on the generations to follow. "My dad did work under the table to provide for many," Mom said. "He taught us that your community is also your family. You must take care of as many people as possible."

My mother was fearless. She could have stayed at home, but she was a champion swimmer who decided to go to the local university. "By 1956, students were making signs, dangerous ones, that read, *"Free Hungary! Russians Go Home."* The students demanded their right to freedom of speech. Mom remembers that a friend was walking near her with a sign. She turned around when she heard gunshots ripping through the air. "My friend disappeared, and when I looked down, I saw that she was gone," Mom said. "They shot her."

That night, my mother left her family, her home, the only life she knew behind to immigrate to Canada with her swim team. It made sense because Mom was training to be an Olympic swimmer and was on top of her game. In 1956, Canada represented an escape from a country in the midst of a massive revolution, where they faced daily dangers.

"To come to Canada, we had to find a way across the Austrian border," Mom said. "It was very scary when we made that crossing. I was walking and crying, walking and crying. "I knew it was either the start of a new life or the end of my life," she said.

In the end, both of my parents escaped Hungary and started again in a new country where they didn't know a soul and couldn't speak a word of English. They had backpacks strapped to their bodies, no jobs, no money, and some very big dreams.

My admiration for them is endless, and I thank them for the Rockstar DNA.

Fast-forward to my own family life.

My parents learned the language, opened their first restaurant, worked in the hospitality industry, and had two daughters, including yours truly and my older sis, Cathi. At one point, a close family friend ended up screwing them over for money, and they lost everything, including their money and the restaurant. I knew we were at risk for losing our home, but they always made it seem as if it was just another obstacle we would conquer. They had already survived so much worse. There was only one thing to do, which was to start again. My parents were pros at it.

Their marriage wasn't perfect. Both dabbled in drinking to combat PTSD, life stressors, raising a family, and, of course, money issues. There were loving moments combined with bitter fights. One thing they did agree upon was that we would be raised with strict rules. You didn't question who was the boss in my early family. He was sitting at the kitchen table, ready to stare you down if you came home late. He would eventually put a military-style bulletin board inside the front door when we were teens, for everyone to see, of all our wrongdoings (lol!). He marked if we came home late, if we smelled like alcohol, and who we went out with that night.

But as a little girl, we lived in a small one-bedroom apartment on Christie Street in midtown. At age four, we moved to Etobicoke to a larger three-bedroom home with a pool in the backyard. We never lacked for anything. Sis and I were raised to have that old-school work mentality. It was so incredibly important to my parents to understand what hard work was all about. There was not much time for loafing around the house or watching TV. We had our chores and were taught early on that life was always about lending a hand to others in need.

We were never home alone.

When I was a little girl, my super strict dad brought his mother, Anna, from Hungary to live with us. My grandmother was six-foot-three, ginormous, and quite strict while also loving us to pieces. She moved here at age seventy to be close to her family. She had strong views, such as she shunned my mother for never having boys. (I guess I made up for that one, as I was branded the boy, but more on that in a minute.) To make up for the lack of little dudes, I acted as the boy my father never had in life.

"I want to play Barbies," my sister would yell.

"No," I'd state. "Let's build something with a hammer and nails, like a doghouse."

I was so ambitious! So, like my father.

The struggle is part of your story. If you're struggling—good. You're in the part of the story where the hero becomes who they were meant to be.

Getting through it—that's where the power is. I learned resilience at a very young age. It's kind of funny: when my friends and I were little and gathered around, they'd talk about their mothers reading stories of *Cinderella* and *Snow White and the Seven Dwarfs*. I was told stories about the Hungarian Revolution—how my mother and her family survived, and what they had to do to make it to the other side. That shaped how I looked at resilience. I didn't look at it as a choice. For me, it was just how life worked.

But what every story they told me had in common was that, on the other side of the obstacle, there is growth. There are lessons, yes—but first and foremost, there's growth. Growth builds character. And I loved hearing the stories of how they overcame, how they pushed, how they endured.

My mother, father, sister, and I were always close. They taught me: *You're going to fall down. Get up, wipe off your knees, shoulders back, chin up, and keep moving forward, no matter what.*

You don't ever stay down for long. You stay down as long as it takes to catch your breath. And if I asked, "How many more minutes am I going to feel this way?" The answer was always, "However long it takes."

They taught me that resilience has no timeline and that I should give myself the grace and space to get through it.

My parents' identity, what they modeled, was turning trauma into growth. That's when I started realizing: what you put *into* trauma is what you'll get out of it.

For some people, trauma equals devastation. That's not how it was for me. I inherited generational trauma. That's science now—it's in your DNA. In my twenties, I wanted to erase that. I wanted to get over how they handled things. It wasn't a *Leave It to Beaver* household, but they worked hard. And they were always there. I always knew I was loved.

When I became a parent, I quickly understood that my parents did the best they could, given their circumstances. To be honest, all things considered, my parents did an awesome job. I had a strong, loving family behind me, even if it wasn't always one hundred percent "healthy." Accepting them as they were—good, bad, indifferent—I was finally able to forgive them. Like when they sent me to kindergarten with not a single word of English beyond "hi." And because I could not communicate with anybody, I was ostracized. Bullied, actually—probably up until tenth grade. I even tried switching schools instead of owning who I was.

And that's why I believe embracing imperfection is a superpower. We're all perfectly imperfect.

Looking back, I can see how their imperfection shaped my empathy. They had suffered incredible losses. They stood in food lines because all their money was taken from them. They had friends and family shot down in front of them. Yet they worried about feeding not only themselves but also their neighbors.

They taught me the power of empathy. That quality has stayed at the top of my values list.

Even today, when somebody wrongs me, I try to remember: That's someone's little boy or little girl. That's someone who probably had their own trauma. You never really know someone else's story.

When I didn't speak English, I observed people. I studied them. Ironically, that became the foundation for what I would do professionally for a few decades.

I became the first female private investigator in North America and have owned my business for over twenty years. Human behavior fascinates me. People live and act based on what they know and what they've experienced, and that's different for everyone. That is why I believe we should always lead with empathy.

Despite their flaws, my parents knew what it took to keep going in the wake of trauma. They dealt with it the best they could. Today, we call it "post-traumatic stress disorder (PTSD)." Back then, they just called it life.

They raised us in a foreign land, navigating a new language and a different culture, while their kids adopted new values and new ideas. It was disorienting for *all* of us.

In those initial years in Canada, their world shrank to a routine of work, school, and groceries, leaving their work in social justice behind.

Our family *was* their social life. But underneath the surface, they were practicing something powerful: self-care and self-preservation.

I didn't grow up with Rockstars, but in many ways, it felt like I did.

Grade school and middle school were a bit of a nightmare. Popular? Please. I was bullied and threatened on a regular basis. That is most definitely a story for a whole other book.

Grade nine wasn't so great. My two besties were a year younger than me, and I still hadn't hit puberty. I got bullied quite a bit because I was so flat, I could have been a boy.

I'd also meet some of my best friends in high school and learn some valuable lessons about people. I was also schooled in how life segregates us into groups. There were the rockers, the funkers, the stoners, the punkers, the jocks, the preppies, the car guys... the list goes on and on. You had to pick a group and stick with it. I decided I wasn't going to do that, and I would be in as many groups as possible. My idea was not welcome at first, but because I was so popular, I was able to do whatever I wanted. I was able to introduce people from one group to another and watched them become the best of friends. No labels. No genders. No boundaries.

I had my two besties, Gina and Nicole—my girls. Gina even works with me now. She is my right-hand, senior case manager, and someone I couldn't live without. Little did I know then that we'd always be together through breakups, bad hairdos, poor relationship choices, divorces, and children. We're still together.

My parents saw right through our tough rocker girl act.

"Where are all the forks?" my dad would ask us.

Dad was a keen observer as we did wear our jeans so tightly that we had to sit on the bed, get one foot in while another girl held the top open, and then wiggle until we could get the other foot in. Also, you had to put a fork into the zipper and bend the shit out of that eating tool in order to zip up the pants, thus melding them to our inner organs. Forks would go missing in the house because, after a few uses, they were so bent that they were unusable for eating.

Our look was completed by big, ZZ Top–style hair and our new boobs. We'd joyride listening to Mötley Crüe, hair glued into place with spray, and our neon-colored '80s zip-up jackets blowing in the breeze. We were cool girls, damn it.

I wish someone had told my parents how cool girls needed to be at all the parties and dances. I wasn't allowed to go anywhere or do anything, and I wasn't even permitted to go to high school dances for long. I got maybe an hour or an hour and a half, and that was before all the good stuff happened.

I was nearly twenty when my parents sat my sister and me down because they had to tell us something. They were nervous and sweating. I thought someone was sick, or dying, or that they were getting divorced. But instead, they told us that my grandmother, my mother's mother, was Jewish, which meant we were Jewish, too. Then, they told us she had to convert to Roman Catholicism, or they would have killed her.

To me, it wasn't shocking. But to them, it was trauma.

They continued the story to tell us that while my mother's family had been wealthy, they lost everything—their home, their belongings. And yet, they were okay because they had each other.

The values they instilled in us were rooted in survival. Fear-based, even. And it took years of therapy and self-realization for me to truly understand how their trauma had shaped them and my sister and me.

They didn't even leave Hungary together. They met in Canada. And they built quite a life.

I have "The struggle is part of the story" tattooed on my body because it is just part of the story. But it is not the whole story. To me, trauma, sadness, and suffering mean you're alive. You have had the privilege to love and experience. You can choose to attach negativity to your story. Or you can choose to say, "This is part of my life."

As a private investigator, I've served thousands of people over the past two decades. Beyond infidelity and custody battles and missing children—even the death of children—I've seen resilience. People taught me what it means to be "okay" in the face of horrific experiences.

It's what you choose to do with those experiences that defines your future.

There are no perfect people. No perfect lives. There are no good guys or bad guys when it comes to trauma. There are just a lot of hard truths and work that needs to be done in order to get through it.

Resilience doesn't arrive wrapped in motivation quotes or polished moments. It's built in the real, the raw, and the reckoning. These are the truths I've learned—not from a textbook, but from rising through what tried to break me. If you're in it right now, this list is for you. Keep it close. Read it when the world gets loud. These are the reminders that carried me—and they'll carry you too.

WHAT I KNOW FOR SURE ABOUT RESILIENCE

- *You don't build resilience when life is calm. You build it when everything's breaking.* Most people wait for peace to find their power, but real strength is forged in the chaos. Resilience is born when you choose to keep going, even when nothing makes sense yet.
- *Confidence isn't something you're handed. It's something you create daily.* You won't wake up one day magically fearless. Confidence grows when you do the hard thing, even when you're afraid, again and again, until you start trusting yourself.
- *The turning point is usually silent.* There's no big moment. It's not loud. It's when you whisper to yourself, "I'm done living like this," and that tiny decision changes everything.
- *Fear doesn't mean stop. It means there's something worth doing.* Waiting until you're "ready" is a trap. Move while scared. The power shows up in the doing, not the doubting.

- *Struggle doesn't mean failure — it means you're in training.* Hard seasons don't mean you're broken. They mean you're being rebuilt. The mess is not the ending. It's the foundation.
- *Outgrowing people and versions of yourself is not betrayal — it's growth.* You are not here to shrink to keep others comfortable. Release the things (and people) that can't rise with you.
- *Resting is not quitting. It's preparing.* If you push through everything, you burn out. The pause is where you recharge your power, not where it disappears.
- *Holding it all in doesn't make you strong — speaking your truth does.* Resilience isn't silence. It's using your voice with intention. Powerfully. Truthfully. Even if it shakes.
- *Boundaries aren't rejection. They're protection.* You teach people how to treat you by what you allow. Boundaries are the blueprint for your next level.
- *You'll never feel fully ready. But you are already equipped.* The world doesn't need a perfect version of you. It needs the real one, right now. Show up as her.

Our experiences are a part of who we are. We move through both internal and external struggles—messy, dramatic, raw. The ups and downs may stem directly from trauma or from how we feel in the moment. Either way, the struggle is real. But accepting the struggle is the first step forward. You can't erase the shitty things that happened to you. You can't undo the ways you've screwed up.

It is what it is. Bad things happen—to good people, too.

Your trauma isn't your *whole* story. But it *is* part of your story. And it makes you who you are today and who you will become tomorrow.

You don't need perfect conditions to rise. You rise because you decide to. Resilience is a practice. A promise you keep to yourself, especially when no one else is watching. It's what separates the women who hope for change from the ones who *create* it.

If you're waiting for the fear to disappear before you move, you'll wait your whole life. Resilience isn't about feeling fearless. It's about moving forward anyway. It's the belief that you don't have to be ready; you just have to be *real*.

You don't need to be the loudest, the fastest, or the most polished. You just need to keep showing up. Fully. Boldly. Unapologetically. Every time you rise after the fall, you prove you are resilient. You are the evidence. You are the power. And if you've been waiting for a sign, this is it.

You're not just part of the Resilience Revolution.

You *are* the revolution.

ROCKSTAR RECAP

Resilience isn't just about surviving; it is about becoming your true, authentic self through the chaos. Your story is valid, and your pain can be a catalyst for a whole different life steeped in love and strength.

Journal Prompts For Readers

- ★ What part of your past have you been ashamed to talk about?

  _____
  _____
  _____
  _____

- ★ How can your family's story be reframed as a story of survival and strength?

  _____
  _____
  _____
  _____

- ★ In what ways have you already proven you're resilient?

  _____
  _____
  _____
  _____

Make Your Move
Write a letter to your younger self, thanking them for surviving the things that tried to break you.

CHAPTER THREE
REJECTION IS REDIRECTION

"The only thing that's keeping you from getting what you want is the story you keep telling yourself."
~ Tony Robbins

Resilience isn't loud. It starts in the quiet moments, when no one claps, and you rise anyway.

In eleventh grade, when everyone was excitedly talking to their guidance counselors about the future, some dreaming of being doctors, accountants, and fashion designers, I was in my element.

My dad always told me I would make a perfect lawyer. He said, "You always have the information. You debate like a pro. You present your ideas so well. And let's not talk about your arguing skills. You should be a lawyer."

I agreed. I always found the law fascinating, and I loved helping others. I definitely wanted to be a lawyer. I remember walking into my guidance counselor's office—shoulders back, chin up—so proud to share my dream.

"I want to be a lawyer," I said.

But he laughed, and not kindly. He laughed in my face and told me I was not smart enough. I didn't have the marks or the ability. He told me not only was I not smart enough, but I wasn't strong enough. He suggested that I should go find a man to take care of me, marry rich, and have children, and I would be fine. Then he dismissed me.

I was shattered. I went home devastated and cried for weeks. I felt crushed, small, and erased. I felt—*not good enough*. And when my parents asked what I said back, I had to admit I just said, "Okay."

They were furious. "Why the hell would you say that? That's not okay. He doesn't get to decide who you become."

They reminded me that if I needed better marks, there was a workaround. There's always a workaround. I needed to work harder or try a different way. They reminded me to never, ever let anyone decide who I was or who I would become.

They may not have had all the answers, but they certainly knew that others didn't have the right to decide my future or my dreams. They made that abundantly clear.

It was that continuous message: It's okay to fail, but when you fall, get up and keep moving forward. That's what matters. It's not the how. It's not the outside influences. It is the belief you have in yourself.

That moment of rejection could've defined me. I could've let it steer me toward the life he thought I was destined for. I could've accepted the narrative someone else handed me.

But I didn't.

I gave myself the space to be crushed and the grace to feel the sting of rejection. But not forever. I didn't camp out in pain. I took a breath, refocused, and marched right back into that office.

"I *want* to be a lawyer," I told him.

No one told me how to upgrade my courses or pivot my plan. My parents, as immigrants, didn't know the system. But they taught me to *figure it out*. I quickly learned that there are ninety-nine solutions for every single problem. The odds were in my favor.

Rejection isn't a dead end—it's a detour toward something bigger, bolder, and more aligned.

I've been told "no" more times than I can count. Doors slammed in my face. Emails ignored. Rooms I wasn't "invited" to. Spaces that didn't welcome me. And every single time, I let it *fuel* me, not *fool* me. Because here's the truth: Rejection doesn't mean you're not good enough. It means you're being redirected to a place where your power can't be ignored.

Every "no" carved the path to a louder "hell yes!" Every setback sharpened my edge. I didn't shrink; I shifted. I didn't retreat; I recalibrated. Because when you're unbreakable, you don't need approval. You just need alignment. And if a door slams shut, trust that you're being pushed toward building your own—bigger, better, and wide open.

As the founder of a private investigation agency, I would often hear my clients tell me they've been rejected, broken up with by their spouse, or robbed by a business partner. My response to them is always the same—"Amazing!" Without fail, they look at me like I've lost my mind. But it's always followed by one of my many mantras: rejection is redirection; "no" means not now, not for you, or not today. Almost always, people are able to process that there's a different plan for the situation.

Many people automatically view rejection as something incredibly negative. It makes them feel bad, emotionally distressed, as though they had done something wrong. But I've learned there is magic in being able to reframe words that are attached to feelings. Words have power. They often shape how we feel about an experience, how we move through it, and how we internalize that.

Tony Robbins taught me the power of language and how it fuels emotion. Change your words, and you change your life.

Lose a client? Awesome.

Partner breaks up with you? Perfect.

Someone ghosted you? Wonderful.

Rejection tried to break me, but it built me instead

- *They said "no."* I thought it meant I wasn't good enough. But that "no" wasn't personal—it was directional. It pushed me into a room I never would've entered if they said "yes." And that room? That's where I rose.
- *I wasn't invited.* At first, it stung. Then I realized—I don't need an invite to build my own table. Rejection forced me to lead instead of wait. It made me own my power instead of asking for space.
- *I gave everything and still got overlooked.* I thought effort guaranteed results. It doesn't. But rejection taught me that alignment matters more than applause. Now, I don't chase rooms. I choose them.
- *They didn't see my value.* So I stopped performing for people who were never qualified to validate me. Rejection taught me to stop proving and start building.
- *Being left out felt like a loss.* But loss is often the very thing that clears the space for expansion. Rejection made me bolder. It showed me I didn't need to be included—I needed to lead.
- *Their silence made me question everything.* Until I realized silence is also an answer. Rejection gave me clarity. It taught me that my next level wouldn't come from being chosen—it would come from choosing myself.
- *I thought rejection was the end of the road.* It wasn't. It was a fork in the road. One path led to playing small. The other led to everything I've built since. I took the one they tried to block—and I made it mine.

- *I believed rejection was failure.* But it was actually the filter. The moment I stopped seeing it as a setback, I saw it for what it was: the beginning of something that could only be built by someone unshakable.

Once you're able to look at it with a clear head, you'll realize that that wasn't for you. Because the story you tell yourself becomes your choice, you can choose to stay sitting in your poopy diaper, or you can choose to rise above the external noise of it. The truth is, more times than not, something better is coming. Often, it's not about finding out the answer, because once you learn what *doesn't* work, you are one step closer to what actually *does*.

When I was younger, failure felt like doom and gloom because I perceived it as negative. Today, I see what is on the other side—the gift in the rubble, the wisdom in the mess, the growth through the chaos.

You won't always be able to see it right away. In the thick of it, it just hurts. But the sheer knowing that there is better on the other side is magical, to say the least. Because once the storm clears, even a little, you'll be able to ask the right questions.

What did this teach me?
Where is this trying to take me?
What door is opening because this one just slammed shut?
Rejection is redirection.

As a private investigator, I've walked with people through their worst nightmares. No one calls a PI because life is good. It's custody battles. Infidelity. Betrayals. Missing people. Devastating truths. What I know for sure is that when somebody comes to me to find answers about someone else, what they ultimately find is the truth about themselves. And that is a power move!

Sometimes, rejection is the beginning of self-clarity and confidence. They begin to investigate important data about how they got there. *Why did I put up with this for so long? Why didn't I expect that person to treat me with kindness and respect? What was my part in this?* Sometimes what looks like the end is actually the start of everything authentic.

So I don't fear failure. I welcome it.

I don't shrink from rejection. I study it.

And I don't let closed doors stop me. I build new ones.

Similar to confidence, resilience isn't taught—it happens in the trenches, in the pain, and in the chaos. It is born the moment you decide, I am not letting this destroy me. There is typically a small window where life can go either way. It happens when those nagging questions come in. *Do I let this experience define who I am and who I will become? How badly do I want this? Why am I giving my power away?* It is not that moment when you decide that you will not let any singular experience define you. It is when you stop shrinking and start *leading like a legend—that's when resilience is unleashed.*

Let's talk about my media company. As the founder of I Am Unbreakable, I am fortunate to lead, elevate, and champion these Rockstar female founders, disruptors, and changemakers. In my opinion, these entrepreneurs are true heroes. They pitch bold ideas, raise capital, create groundbreaking products, and flip industries on their heads—and do it in heels, sneakers, or cowboy boots.

They don't ask for permission. They walk into rooms that were not built for them. They raise capital. They own the stage. And guess what? If there is a stage where they belong, they build it, and then, *they own it.*

You don't need to play small. You need to be undeniable. Unstoppable and unapologetically you. *On purpose!*

This is Rockstar Confidence.

It's your edge. Your fuel. Your fire.

Rejection didn't break me—it built me.

Every door that closed taught me how to kick down the next one.

Every "no" taught me to stop asking for permission.

Rejection stripped away the noise and the detours—and forced me to get crystal clear on who I am and what I'm here to do.

I stopped waiting to be chosen and chose *myself.*

I stopped seeing setbacks as stop signs and started seeing them as part of the strategy.

I stopped trying to achieve perfection and started showing up authentically.

When they didn't get it? That was my cue to move on and *be bolder*.

When they counted me out? That was when I counted *myself* in.

Rejection isn't failure.

Redirection isn't a loss.

Rejection is redirection.

It's *opportunity*.

It's *owning your shift*.

It's *alignment*.

It's your next level waiting to be unlocked.

You are not here to be accepted, applauded, and liked by everyone.

You are here to be *undeniable to yourself*.

You are here to win for *you*.

The stage that's meant for you will never require you to shrink. To wear a mask or to pretend to be someone you are not.

And the door that's meant for you? It opens the moment you walk in like a legend, and you know your worth.

And when it does open?

Step through it like the Rockstar you've *always* been.

ROCKSTAR RECAP

Rejection isn't a wall, it's a new opportunity, a shift and a pathway into a different version of your life. Often, one is more aligned with your truth. The key is choosing to walk through it.

Journal Prompts For Readers

★ What was your most painful "no," and where did it ultimately lead you?

_____
_____
_____
_____

★ Who or what have you been trying to earn approval from?

_____
_____
_____
_____

★ What part of your story are you proud of that only exists because of rejection?

_____
_____
_____
_____

Make Your Move
Make a timeline of your rejections, major detours that turned out to be blessings. Share one with someone you trust.

CHAPTER FOUR
MANIFEST LIKE A ROCKSTAR

"You become what you believe."
~ Oprah Winfrey

Manifestation is vision with a backbone—not a wish, but a warning: I'm coming for everything with my name on it. It's about deciding. It's the moment you stop asking for permission and start moving like it's already yours. It doesn't require proof. It requires presence. You don't need to see the finish line to take the first step—you need conviction. The kind that comes from knowing, deep down, that what you feel pulling at you isn't random. It's a calling. And most people ignore it because it's easier to stay where it's safe. But the ones who rise? They follow it—without applause, without certainty, without a guarantee.

Manifestation is the art of holding the door open for the life you haven't lived yet—and walking through it anyway. It's not about asking the universe—it's about becoming undeniable to it.

It's choosing the vision before the evidence. It's speaking what hasn't happened yet, then backing it with action, discipline, and unshakable belief. That's not delusion. That's leadership. The world won't believe it until you do. So believe it. Move. Show up like it's already unfolding—because if you don't, someone else will rise in the space you were meant to own.

You don't need to become someone else to lead. You need to *remember* who you were before the world told you to be quiet. Then you rise, bolder than ever.

I've stood at the edge of the stage—heart pounding, voice shaking—knowing damn well I could fall flat on my face in front of everyone watching. And I walked in anyway.

I showed up for *myself*.

Because here's the truth: If you want to live a bold, purpose-driven life, you have to be willing to get your ass kicked in the process. You don't manifest by standing safely on the sidelines. You manifest by stepping into the ring—messy, unfiltered, and *all in*.

You go after the dream knowing it won't be handed to you. You get strategic. You stay grounded. You build belief and back it with *action*. Manifesting isn't magic—it's guts, clarity, and follow-through. It's discipline. It's asking yourself who you need to become to hold what you're asking for—and then *become her*. You stop looking for guarantees and start building momentum. You stop needing applause and start trusting your own rhythm.

The dream doesn't show up when you're ready—it shows up when you're willing to risk something real for it. And if you're in the arena? Bleeding, sweating, and building something that matters. You're already doing it. That's what manifesting like a Rockstar *actually* looks like.

Manifesting like a Rockstar isn't about wishful thinking—it's about becoming the version of you who already owns the stage. It's vision with *volume*, backed by action, grit, and bold belief. You don't just dream it—you *demand* it, then *do* the damn work. Because Rockstars don't wait for magic—they *are* the magic.

Believe it.
See it.
Live it.

I don't manifest by hoping—I manifest by deciding. Over the years, I've learned that manifestation isn't about waiting for the stars to align. It's about aligning yourself with vision, clarity, and relentless follow-through. It's about trusting your gut, taking the risk, and becoming the version of you who already owns the outcome. I've tested it. I've lived it. And I know what works. So if you're done with surface-level advice and ready to lead with conviction, here's what I know for sure about manifesting like a Rockstar—personally and professionally.

Manifestation, unfiltered. This is what I know for sure.

- *Manifesting like a Rockstar means showing up as the woman who has already built it.* You don't wait to become her—you lead from her.
- *Vision alone isn't enough.* Strategy seals the deal. Dream it, define it, and execute with discipline that matches your ambition.
- *How you show up matters.* Your energy, confidence, and clarity speak louder than any pitch or portfolio.
- *Self-belief is non-negotiable.* In business and in life, no one buys into you if you haven't bought into yourself first.
- *Protect your vision, but don't keep it locked away.* Speak it with intention, build it boldly, and move like it's already real.
- *Manifestation is the inner work behind outer success.* It's how leaders make aligned decisions, build momentum, and trust the process.
- *You won't step into what you won't own.* Name the dream. Claim the title. Lead like you're already holding it.
- *This isn't about waiting.* It's about moving with clarity, purpose, and unshakable belief—even when the results haven't caught up yet.

Growing up, when I was looking for a mentor, I didn't see many women who were strong in the way I wanted to be—until Oprah.

I couldn't get home fast enough to watch her talk shows. The way she connected so authentically and so vulnerably was mind-blowing. She was my hero and my mentor. Oprah was the one who wasn't supposed to succeed for a multitude of reasons. But she never let the outside influences stop her from following her dreams.

I was in my parents' basement trying to figure out what was next. I remember that day like it was yesterday. It was a pivotal time in my life as I was trying to figure out what was next. I had just graduated from high school and was told that I was not smart enough to do what I thought was my dream. I remember exactly how anxious and depressed I felt about myself because I didn't have the answers. But Oprah was coming on soon, and little did I know that the next episode would totally change the trajectory of my life.

It was about being an entrepreneur. Something I had always been interested in, but could never move forward with, as I did not know anything about raising capital or bootstrapping businesses. She said something that day that shifted everything for me. She said, "I know what you're all thinking. It's easy for me to say this because I have money. But where there is a will, there is a way. You don't always need to know your *how*. I know people who risked it all and opened their business by using credit cards."

Well, guess what I did? I got a couple of credit cards, and I opened up my first business. I took a chance on *myself*. That was Rockstar Confidence in action. I didn't know the exact *how*, but I knew I had to try because Oprah said I could. And how did she connect with her audience? Authentically, vulnerably, with kindness and love, with the purpose of serving others.

She is *the* resilience queen. They told her she'd never make it because she was a woman of color. People ridiculed her weight. And still, she rose.

Her story of pain, rejection, and rising anyway was the story I needed to hear. Decades ago, she shared it with the world, long before "vulnerability" and "authenticity" were buzzwords. She was real, and that made her *undeniable*.

That's when I knew: I want to be like her when I grow up.

Today, in Chapters and Indigo bookstores across the country, my magazine, *I Am Unbreakable,* sits right beside Oprah's. In my very first issue, I manifested that I was going to interview three powerhouse women. One of them, of course, is Oprah.

I've already interviewed two of the three women I listed—Shelly Zalis and Lisa Bilyeu. Oprah, if you're reading—I've got one more to go, lol. The funny thing is, I have never reached out to anyone on her team because I strongly believe it will be in a different, more organic way. Before finishing this book, it became crystal clear. I saw her interview Mel Robbins about her book, *The Let Them Theory*. Let the manifestation begin.

I'll keep you posted on the interview.

The influence of positive affirmation on our mental landscape and emotional well-being cannot be overstated. The evidence I've collected and experienced over my lifetime makes it undeniable. I can say without a doubt and with one thousand percent certainty that manifestation is real, and for me, it works every single time.

Every time we consciously tell ourselves things like *I can do anything,* we are engaging in a powerful act of self-affirmation. Research shows that this practice can profoundly shape our thoughts, emotions, and behaviors, leading to a more positive and empowered mindset.

At the core of this practice lie two simple yet profound words: *I am.* These words hold the key to unlocking our inherent qualities, strengths, and aspirations. By combining positive affirmation with *I am,* we are making a deliberate and intentional choice to focus on statements that uplift and empower us.

Ultimately, the practice of affirmation is linked to the concept of manifestation, or the idea that our thoughts and beliefs have the power to shape our reality. By consistently affirming positive statements such as "I am confident," "I am loved," "I am okay," "I am worthy," we are aligning our inner beliefs with our desired outcomes, thus setting the stage for these manifestations to become realities in our lives.

Regularly affirming these positive statements can have a transformative impact on our sense of self-worth, resilience, and outlook on life. This practice serves as an antidote to negative self-talk and self-doubt and nurtures a deep well of confidence and belief within ourselves. Embracing the power of *I am* and integrating positive affirmations into our daily lives fosters a supportive internal dialogue. The shift in self-talk can significantly enhance our mental and emotional well-being, boosting our motivation and fostering a profound sense of personal empowerment.

Same with my three favorite words: *Yes, You Can*.

Manifestation is moving in alignment before the world gives you approval, because your future doesn't need permission. It's the moment you stop negotiating with fear and start executing like it's already happening.

When you want something badly, you need to become obsessed with it. And by obsessed, I mean that everything in your body, soul, and mind has to be fully committed.

I am obsessed with being disciplined. I am obsessed with my work ethic. I am obsessed with outworking everyone. I am curious. I am open. Clearly, I believe in the *I am* affirmation, which is where I Am Unbreakable came from. I found it to be a very powerful affirmation during the times I am in the chaos.

Manifestation is not achieved by waving a magic wand. However, I often ask my clients, "If I had a magic wand and could give you anything your heart desires, what would it be?" Some say they'd want a thriving business, to which I ask them what they're doing to make that happen.

One of my favorite quotes from Brené Brown is, "For something new to be born, something else has to die." If you want to be a professional athlete, you have to say goodbye to the couch, the party life, the "I want and chips." If you want your business to make $5 million, you have to say goodbye to comfort and certainty.

Big dreams require big trade-offs. Small dreams, small ones. But there's always a trade-off.

I believe we're energy. Our thoughts attract what we get. That's why I changed *rejection* to *redirection*. Rejection feels final, but redirection? That's strategy.

When you shift your thoughts, you shift your outcomes. I've seen addicts heal, broken people rise, and very unhealthy people live their best lives. It all transformed for them when they allowed themselves to believe in something greater—God, the universe, their own soul—they found a higher power and turned their lives around.

Manifestation doesn't remove pain. It helps you move through it. When you suffer, when life gets hard and you fall, your mindset and focus determine—*if you rise*. So if you believe this to be true, that means that you do have and control your power.

You're no longer trying to convince—you're just creating.

HERE ARE MY EIGHT POWERFUL INDICATORS THAT MANIFESTATION IS UNFOLDING:

1. **You're no longer trying to convince—you're just creating.**
   The energy of proving has been replaced with the clarity of building. You're not chasing. You're calling it in.
2. **The vision feels bigger than you, and that excites you.**
   You're not intimidated by the stretch. You're ready for it. You're not shrinking to fit old stories anymore.
3. **You're being tested right before the breakthrough.**
   Everything is showing up to ask, "Are you sure you want this?" And your answer is unwavering.

4. **You're saying "no" faster and without guilt.** You've stopped making space for what drains you. You're protecting your energy like it's sacred currency—because it is.
5. **You're obsessed with who you're becoming.** Not the outcome, not the timeline—the *you* that's emerging in the process. That's where the power lives.
6. **The "old you" feels like a different lifetime.** You can't unsee your growth. You're responding differently, thinking bigger, and walking taller—even if no one else sees it yet.
7. **Your inner dialogue is sharper, stronger, cleaner.** You've stopped negotiating with doubt. You're speaking to yourself like someone who's already there.
8. **You feel the edge, and you're not backing away.** You're standing in it. Eyes open. Shoulders back. Knowing damn well that edge is the gateway to everything you asked for.

I'm not going to lie—sometimes it's very hard. But during those times, I remind myself: *I don't know why I'm going through this. It's horrendous. It's painful and awful. But I'll get through it. And I always do. Not because I had a vision board, but because I believe in myself and trust the process.*

As humans, we love. As humans, we suffer. We can't escape that. And I don't think most of us would want to—because we wouldn't suffer if we didn't love. I believe it's the trade-off.

Renowned 19th-century British poet Alfred Lord Tennyson wrote, *"Tis better to have loved and lost than never to have loved at all."*

It is not just about hoping things will happen or believing in it. It's understanding what manifesting is and knowing it isn't a wish. It's the process of becoming who we truly are and then working to make it happen. It's getting comfortable with our discomfort, knowing that if something needs to change, we have the power to change it.

I think about Jim Carrey's story. At one point, he was homeless and starving. But as a believer in manifestation, he wrote himself a check for $1 million and kept it in his wallet. A few months later, he landed the role in *The Mask*, and life as he knew it changed for the better.

Similarly to Jim, every single thing I've built started with belief... *and then I went to work*. Rockstars don't wait for magic—they realize *they are* the magic. You don't need to prove your worth—you need to activate it.

So, name the vision. Build the plan. Show up like it already belongs to you. Because if you can see it, and you're willing to work for it, you're already halfway there.

This is manifesting like a Rockstar.

Manifestation isn't about waiting. It's about rising. It's about becoming the version of you who doesn't just dream it but moves like it's non-negotiable. The truth is, everything you want is already circling you. It's not a matter of if—it's a matter of *alignment*. The vision didn't come to you by accident. You were chosen to carry it. To birth it. To back it with grit, clarity, and resilience, no one can shake loose. This chapter? It's not about manifesting a moment. It's about building a life that reflects what you *knew* before the world could see it.

Keep showing up.

Keep choosing.

Keep becoming.

Because the future isn't waiting, it's watching to see if you're really ready to claim it.

ROCKSTAR RECAP

Manifestation isn't magic, although it can be. It's vision, plus clarity, plus relentless action, built brick by brick—for you. It is living, breathing, and believing you are already there.

Journal Prompts For Readers

★ What is one bold outcome you're currently manifesting?

_____
_____
_____
_____

★ What's holding you back from believing it's possible?

_____
_____
_____
_____

★ What is one small action you can take today to align with that vision?

_____
_____
_____
_____

Make Your Move
Write your vision in the present tense as if it were already true and place it somewhere visible for thirty days.

CHAPTER FIVE
THE THREE F-BOMBS

*"Think like a queen. A queen is not afraid to fail.
Failure is another stepping stone to greatness."*
~ Oprah Winfrey

Wear failure like battle scars. Don't fear the fall—own the comeback.

The Three F-Bombs—**Fear, Failure, and Forgiveness**—aren't setbacks; they're *power moves* when you flip the script. Fear isn't your enemy—it's your fuel. Failure isn't the end—it's the backstage pass to your breakthrough. And forgiveness? That's how you drop the weight and rise bolder, lighter, and legendary.

When I talk about F-bombs, people always get nervous—because anyone who knows me knows I'm not opposed to dropping a few in a conversation. But this time, we're talking about something different: the three f-bombs that stop people from living their dreams.

The first one is **Fear**. It's a sneaky little bugger. Fear plays a mean game of hide and seek. I love to refer to fear as:

- False
- Evidence
- Appearing
- Real.

Fear often doesn't show up waving a flag. It can disguise itself as stress, anxiety, depression, anger, or frustration. When we get scared, we might lash out or shut down. Fight or flight mode kicks in. It's the body's way of protecting itself, often paralyzing us from moving forward. But it's in these moments that we have to be vulnerable enough to acknowledge the fear is there and begin sifting through what's real and what's not.

I'm not saying it's easy. Trust me—been there, done that, got the T-shirt… several actually. Every now and then, life humbles us. But if we let fear win, it starts to own every thought, every move—and that is not a good place to live.

As I shared earlier in the book, when I was struggling to find a mentor, I was fortunate enough to connect with Tony Robbins, from whom I learned two of the most important lessons I still swear by and tell anyone who'll listen.

The first was during a time when I was going through some really heavy personal and family stuff. I remember it like yesterday—I was extremely upset. And he looked at me and said with his deep, convincing voice, "You get what you tolerate." I was floored. This was someone I admired, trusted, and he was essentially telling me that I got what I deserved. I left that event and went completely radio silent.

About six months later, someone from his office called me. I shared what happened. She laughed. When I asked why she laughed, she said something similar had happened to her. At that point, I thought, *Man, this Tony Robbins guy has some nerve.* But then she asked if I'd heard what he said after that. I said "no"—I had been too mortified to stick around. She told me I missed one of his biggest teachings: "You get what you tolerate, so raise your standards."

That changed so much for me. But back then, I wasn't ready to hear it. I wasn't ready to listen. Once I did, though, I didn't just raise my standards—I learned about the power of listening.

I started attending all his events again. Another day, he looked me square in the eye and said, "You were made for the big stage."

And I literally laughed out loud. I told him, "I'm the girl who skipped school every time there were class speeches. I'm terrified of public speaking. It will never happen."

But I remembered the mistake I made last time—preemptively leaving—so this time, I led with curiosity instead. Knowing my fear, I asked him why he would say that. His response was so powerful: "It's usually the thing you fear the most that you actually want the most." Tony said.

One thing that's always helped me, especially as a former private investigator, is the acronym F.E.A.R. I'm all about evidence. So I started investigating: *Is what I'm thinking really true? Where's the proof? What are the odds this will actually happen?* I evaluate from there. If there's actual evidence, maybe it's not just fear—maybe it's something I need to examine and deal with. Shift. Pivot. Adjust.

My second F-bomb is **Forgiveness**.

Especially in the face of trauma or tragedy, forgiveness can feel impossible.

We forgive others all the time, so why is it so hard to forgive ourselves? Why is it so hard to give ourselves when forgiveness is one of the highest forms of self-love? As Brené Brown prompts us to consider, what is it that must die within us before we can forgive?

Forgiveness is one of the most generous gifts you can give yourself. But it doesn't always mean calling up someone who hurt you to say, "I forgive you."

For me, I often forgave people for what they did, and they didn't even know. If you can give yourself the *grace* to let something go because the weight will be less on you, then do it. There is a magical power in the forgiveness that you grant yourself.

My last F-bomb—my favorite—is **Failure**.

People are so damn terrified of failing. But failure isn't the enemy. It's the teacher. It's the redirection. And it's what most people run from. Whether it's a failed test, a relationship, a job, or a business—it doesn't matter. We make up stories: *If I fail, I'll look stupid. Everyone will know. It'll be all over school... or work... or social media... or the news.* But unless you're an A-list celebrity, I promise—it's not making the front page. And if for some reason it does, it will be short-lived.

Melanie Perkins, the founder of Canva, was rejected over 100 times by investors, yet she didn't stop at the tenth rejection. She *kept going*. She took feedback. She tuned out the noise. She made it her superpower. She asked questions, evaluated, and improved. That's what failure teaches you. There is always growth on the other side of failure.

Too many people don't start something new—not a business, not a relationship, not a dream—because they're afraid to fail. But isn't it better to have tried and failed than not to have ever tried at all?

At the end of life, people don't think, *I wish I had worked more.* They think, *I wish I had lived. I wish I had tried.* So I made a decision: I would *welcome* failure into my life. I wouldn't let it dictate my future. I reframed it.

Failure just means you need a new approach. Try again. Shift. Zig when you thought you were going to zag. And even if you fail over and over, what you gain in growth, in grit, and in clarity is invaluable.

As you've learned by now, rejection is redirection. "No" might mean "not right now" or "not this path," and that's okay. It's in these moments that resilience is born and confidence is forged.

I've lived these F-bombs. Deeply.

More than eighteen years ago, I met my forever husband, Matt. I truthfully don't remember meeting him at an event. It was something like that, right? All I knew was he was kind, handsome, fun, and patient. He came from an amazing family. His parents accepted our relationship, and I love them dearly. Matt is a solid, good man who was immediately present for my boys, which was wonderful. We welcomed our fourth son into the world shortly after we said I do. It was an incredible time. A police detective with a warm heart and sharp mind, he loved me and the four boys. We could talk about anything and had tons of fun together.

But I could always sense something was off with him. A sense of sadness would come over him. As an acting police sergeant, I assumed it was part of the job. Well, that's what Google said anyway. Shortly after he left policing, he was diagnosed with PTSD. I was terrified. I didn't understand it. I was raising four kids and running businesses. I was scared every day. We talked. A lot. And for years, we didn't know what it was. The road was long. And it cost him. *It cost us and our boys.*

He worked so hard to get better. And I fought beside him. But yes, there was a deep fear that we wouldn't make it. And that's where forgiveness became everything.

It was the deal-breaker: not just forgiving him but wholly surrendering to what I could not control. It was also imperative that I forgive myself for not knowing sooner, for struggling to keep it all together, for feeling frustrated and defeated.

Forgiveness freed me.

We both gave up everything—his stable career as a police sergeant, my successful PR firm. We had four little kids. It felt like jumping out of a plane without a parachute.

At one point, we were digging under car seats for change just to buy a coffee at Tim Hortons. And then—there it was. A $5 bill. We cried like we won the lottery. I still have that bill framed on our wall to remind me that when you're in the trenches, if you have the right people around you—and if you have even a spark of belief—you're going to be okay.

While my husband was still dealing with his mental health challenges, I was still raising the four kids, still working, still showing up. The road was extremely bumpy, there were roadblocks, dead ends, and definitely, there were multi-vehicle accidents. And it was freaking hard.

But showing up saved me. And while I was helping others fix themselves, their relationships, their families, I was fighting to save my own.

People said, "You and your husband seem like such a strong couple." Of course we were, but we had no idea what we were walking through.

To bring it back to Tony Robbins, he says, "When you live in gratitude and service, there's no room for depression or anxiety," and I believe this to be true.

Supporting someone through mental illness is a lot. And no one talks about the partner on the other side of that pain.

One day, my therapist told me the oxygen mask story. You know, the one every airline preaches before takeoff: *put on your own mask first.*

I was furious. I said, "No way. My kids come first."

To that, she asked, "Then who's helping them when you're unconscious or worse, dead?"

And that was it. A lightbulb. If I'm not okay, how could I take care of anyone else?

I didn't rise because I was fearless. I rose because I had no choice, and I was beyond exhausted from playing small.

Let's get real. The three F-Bombs will shape your rise more than any win ever will.

Fear? Face it.

Failure? Embrace it.

Forgiveness? This one's for *you*, not them. It's how you cut the dead weight, reclaim your power, and stop carrying what was never yours to hold.

These aren't just hard lessons—they're power moves. The truth is, every woman who's ever built something unstoppable has had to walk through all three. So the next time they show up, don't flinch.

Feel them.

Flip them.

Forge through them.

Fear, Failure, and Forgiveness—the three F-Bombs every leader faces, whether they admit it or not. Fear shows up when you're about to level up. Failure hits when you've risked something real. And forgiveness? That's the hardest flex of all—it's what frees you to rise without dragging the weight of the past behind you. I've walked through all three. They don't go away, but you *can* learn to flip them. These aren't weaknesses. These are *power levers* when you know how to use them. Here's how to shift each one when it tries to keep you small:

FEAR

- You overthink everything and stay stuck in "what ifs." → *Decide fast, adjust later. Clarity comes in motion, not in hesitation.*
- You talk yourself out of opportunities before they begin. → *Back yourself like it's already yours. Confidence is built through action, not perfection.*
- You play small so you won't be judged. → *They're going to judge anyway—might as well give them something real to look at.*
- You wait for fear to go away before moving forward. → *It won't. Do it scared. That's where the real edge is.*

FAILURE

- You tie your self-worth to your results → *Detangle your identity from outcomes. One failed moment doesn't define your rise.*
- You avoid taking risks because you're afraid to fall. → *Reframe risk as data. Every miss gives you what you need to get sharper next time.*
- You carry shame from past mistakes → *Shift from shame to strategy. Ask, "What is this trying to teach me?"*
- You try to bounce back instantly to prove you're okay. → *Honor the fall. Then get up slower, but stronger and smarter.*

FORGIVENESS

- You replay old stories that keep you angry or stuck. → *Rewrite the narrative. Forgiveness isn't about them—it's about freeing you.*
- You try to "move on" without doing the inner work. → *Pause. Process. Release. There's no shortcut to healing that lasts.*
- You blame yourself for not knowing better at the time. → *You know better now. That's what matters. Use it.*
- You think forgiving means forgetting. → *Forgiveness doesn't erase the lesson—it reclaims your power to rise beyond it.*

ROCKSTAR RECAP

Fear, forgiveness, and failure are not your enemies—they are your instructors. Each one teaches you how to be bolder, lighter, and stronger.

Journal Prompts For Readers

★ What is fear disguising itself as in your life right now?

_____

_____

_____

_____

★ Who do you need to forgive to move forward?

_____

_____

_____

_____

★ What has failure taught you that success never could?

_____

_____

_____

_____

Make Your Move
Pick one thing you've been avoiding out of fear and take one brave step toward it today.

CHAPTER SIX
OWN YOUR SHIFT

"Owning your story can be hard, but not nearly as difficult as spending your life running from it."
~ Brené Brown

Owning your shift means standing in your full story, *not just the highlight reel*. It's turning your scars into *the comeback* and your setbacks into strategy opportunities. You don't run from your past—you *rock it* like a crown. Because when you own your shift, you stop hiding and start leading like the legend you are.

Stepping into my role as the founder of a PI firm, I felt like I was finally coming home to the purpose I set out for myself so many years ago as a teenager. I wanted to facilitate justice. But instead of being a lawyer, I realized that I had a different role to play. And to truly lead, especially in a room full of male ex-police officers, sergeants, and detectives, I had to own my shit—and own my shift.

Walking into a very male-dominated space didn't scare me. It didn't even dawn on me to be nervous because I've always believed in doing what you love and loving what you do.

But becoming a leader in a male-dominated industry wasn't what I expected. I thought I'd step in, make a change, be welcomed with open arms, make a difference, help individuals and corporations, and I learned quickly that wasn't exactly the case. I had to really own my shift and embrace what I brought to the table.

Being a woman was an asset. I led with empathy, kindness, and understanding. I was always authentic and truthful, even when it wasn't what they wanted to hear.

The feedback I received was that clients would call other agencies and often get curt, detached responses from men. They didn't feel comfortable opening up or sharing their deepest, darkest secrets with someone who didn't even try to create a sense of safety.

Talking to a PI about personal matters is hard. It's vulnerable. But people told me that I made them feel seen, that I was able to create a safe space almost immediately. Like they belonged. Like they weren't being judged.

Some clients told me it took them weeks, months, even years, to finally make that call. They'd say, "I wish I had done this earlier, but I just didn't feel comfortable. I thought I'd be dismissed. My partner told me I was crazy. Am I?"

And I'd say, "Absolutely not."

That's the space I created. That's what I brought. I know this because nearly every client has told me that.

In a twist of irony, I was eventually welcomed into the industry *because* of my gender. It became my competitive edge. Just like a man entering a female-dominated industry can offer something unique, I knew I brought something innovative and important, too.

Regardless of gender, we all have value to bring. I am a huge believer in allyship. For me, it came down to spotting the gaps and showing up differently.

When people make that tough call, they're not looking for bravado.

They're looking for connection. And our competitors noticed. They saw how much we'd done in such a short time—from branding and marketing to awards and visibility. A lot of it was innovative. Things no one in the industry had done before.

I wasn't just there to make money. I was all about creating relationships. I cared. And that was felt. Women told me they were more comfortable talking to another woman. And, surprisingly, men said the same.

That was a real edge for me.

You don't have to be everything to everyone. You just have to be the best version of *you*.

I know I'm not for everyone. I'm direct. I'm honest. I lead with empathy, but I don't sugarcoat. And just knowing that—*owning that*—is powerful. When you can lay your head down at night and think, *I did my best. I led with love, integrity, and compassion;* that's success.

Some people adore working with me and say I exceed expectations. And others? Not so much. And that's okay. Even Apple has a dissatisfaction rate.

So I remind myself that it's not always about *you*. Often, their dissatisfaction has nothing to do with what you've done and everything to do with what they're going through.

Your mindset is one of your most powerful assets for growth. When you own your shift, you own everything. The good, the bad, the *room for improvement*, and the *you're crushing it* parts. And when you're crushing it, you should be mentoring others to do the same.

Your greatest strength lies just above your shoulders. As you learned in the last chapter, we can manifest change, yes, but not without work. Manifestation must be paired with effort.

Mindset is where discipline lives. And with discipline, the world is yours. Because action, no matter how small, is what sets your future in motion.

I believe this wholeheartedly: If you take action, something always follows. The consequence might be positive or negative, big or small, but movement always creates momentum.

Motion is required—it's the law of nature. A strong mindset is the foundation—it separates the one-percenters.

But mindset alone isn't enough. You need to pair it with action.

There were times in my work as a private investigator when I was truly tested—not just professionally, but emotionally. I remember one woman—let's call her Alice. She was curled up on the floor in the fetal position. Her husband had taken their three kids. He'd pulled legal strings she didn't understand. She wasn't as educated and didn't have the resources.

At that moment, she was falling apart. She told me she was done. That he had the kids, the money, the lawyers, the power. That she'd never win. She was spiraling.

I talked her off the ledge. I didn't promise her an outcome, but I asked her, "What do you want? What do you really want?"

She realized she didn't want the marriage. But she never wanted to lose her children. And he knew that. He used it as a weapon.

She didn't believe she could fight back. But over time, she did.

That's the power of *truth*. Of being honest with yourself. You have to look in the mirror, figuratively or literally, and ask: *Why am I doing this? Who am I doing it for? Where did I learn this? Can I change it?* You have to stop justifying patterns and start understanding them. That's how change happens.

No, it doesn't need to be a massive leap. Tiny steps matter. As long as you're moving forward, you're growing. The problem starts when you stop.

When I was the only woman in the room, I had to dig deep. The rejection I faced wasn't about my skills. It was about my gender.

I had to tune out the noise. The outside influences. The doubts. The people who told me to quit.

I never did, and I never looked back. I learned so much from not quitting, and it was hard. And I mean really hard. There were days that

I wanted to quit so badly. But when your mindset becomes your power, you become unstoppable because you control what you think and believe—no one else.

Owning your shift feels phenomenal. It's freeing. You stop pretending. You stop performing. My bestie, Chris, always says, "When you're trying to be someone else, you'll never be the best version of you." So well said!

Owning your shift is also about being authentic. It's about vulnerability. And it's essential for any leader, any entrepreneur, anyone who wants to create real impact. One reason I believe my businesses thrive is because I connect through realness. It's "I understand. I've been there. I'm in the trenches with you."

To take care of your mindset, you've got to listen to your needs. If that means running your business on a Sunday, do it. If it means sitting in silence for fifteen minutes while someone watches the kids, do that. Listen to what your body and mind are telling you.

Humans fear change. We're wired for comfort. And when you shift, even for the better, your mind pulls you back. It's not telling you it's wrong, just that it's hard.

Tony Robbins talks about the sideways figure eight. When you're moving up—making progress—you feel momentum. Then you hit a dip. Your mind pulls you back to comfort. Often, that's why you think, *Why am I self-sabotaging?* But if you can learn to catch yourself at the dip and keep going, you break the cycle and create sustainable momentum. You hit balance. And when you do, that's mastery.

We all want something to change. Something to be better. But stop wishing, stop dreaming, and start doing.

Owning your shift means you stop pretending, stop polishing, and start telling the whole damn truth. The messy parts. The broken parts. The comeback parts. You don't need to hide the hard chapters—you need to lead with them.

You can avoid your story, or you can own it—but only one leads to freedom. Hiding the hard parts doesn't protect you; it *limits you*. The truth you're afraid to face is the very thing that holds your breakthrough. Owning your shift isn't easy, but living disconnected from your purpose is harder. When you finally step into your full story, no edits, no filters—you stop performing and start *leading*.

Examples of the problem (avoiding the shift):

- You minimize your past to make others comfortable. Meanwhile, it's holding your power hostage.
- You keep chasing the next goal so you don't have to sit with what's unresolved.
- You tell the polished version of your story, but feel disconnected from your own truth.

Takeaway: When you own your shift, you reclaim your voice. You stop hiding behind what happened and start *building from it.* Your scars don't make you less credible—they make you *real.* And in leadership, in life, and in impact, real is what resonates. Owning your story unlocks alignment, authority, and the kind of presence that can't be faked.

Examples of the outcome (owning the shift):

- You no longer carry shame—you carry wisdom, and people feel it when you speak.
- You attract aligned opportunities because your energy isn't divided between who you are and who you pretend to be.
- You show up in rooms differently—clear, grounded, and unapologetically whole.

Here's what that looks like in real life:

- You've gone through betrayal or heartbreak, and you try to numb or avoid the pain → *When you face it head-on, you build unshakable boundaries, radical clarity, and emotional depth that no one can take from you.*
- You're stuck in a version of yourself you've outgrown, afraid of what others will say if you change → *Owning your shift gives you the freedom to evolve, expand, and lead with integrity — not for their approval, but for your alignment.*
- You've been silenced, dismissed, or underestimated, and started believing that story → *Telling your own truth rewrites the narrative. It puts you back in the driver's seat — and others will follow your lead.*
- You keep waiting for the right moment to reinvent yourself → *There is no perfect moment. The shift begins the second you decide you're done shrinking for a life that no longer fits.*

Here's what that looks like in real life:

- You've gone through betrayal or heartbreak, and you try to numb or avoid the pain → *When you face it head-on, you build unshakable boundaries, radical clarity, and emotional depth that no one can take from you.*
- You're stuck in a version of yourself you've outgrown, afraid of what others will say if you change → *Owning your shift gives you the freedom to evolve, expand, and lead with integrity, not for their approval, but for your alignment.*
- You've been silenced, dismissed, or underestimated, and started believing that story → *Telling your own truth rewrites the narrative. It puts you back in the driver's seat — and others will follow your lead.*

- You keep waiting for the right moment to reinvent yourself
  → *There is no perfect moment. The shift begins the second you decide you're done shrinking for a life that no longer fits.*

Your past isn't baggage. It's proof that you've walked through fire and came out with something to say. When you own your story fully, you stop shrinking to fit and start rising to lead. You become your true, authentic self—not because you're perfect, but because you're real. And that's what the world needs more of. Not highlight reels. Honest ones.

So wear the scars. Walk in the lessons. And turn every part of your past into the power you lead with. That's how legends are made.

ROCKSTAR RECAP

Your growth doesn't require permission. When you own your identity, evolution, and mindset, your shift is not just your life, but the lives around you.

Journal Prompts For Readers

- ★ What shift are you currently stepping into?

  _____
  _____
  _____
  _____

- ★ What does unapologetic leadership look like for you?

  _____
  _____
  _____
  _____

- ★ How does your mindset support or sabotage your mission?

  _____
  _____
  _____
  _____

Make Your Move
Declare your next shift out loud, write it down, and tell one trusted person who can hold you accountable.

CHAPTER SEVEN
NICE GUT

"Trust your instincts. Intuition doesn't lie."
~ Oprah Winfrey

That inner voice? It's not random—it's your built-in truth detector. And it *doesn't lie*. Trusting your intuition means leading from instinct, not insecurity. When you stop second-guessing and start listening, you unlock next-level clarity, confidence, and badass decision-making. Your gut doesn't whisper for no reason—it *knows*.

After a few years working as a private investigator, I started to see patterns in people, in relationships, in betrayals, and in all kinds of wild situations. Over time, I noticed something: clients were making the same ill-informed decisions over and over again.

I'd say, "Keep your money. If you think he or she is cheating, they are!" But still, every one of them wanted to pay us to confirm what they already knew in their bones. And 99.9 percent of the time, their gut had been right all along.

Just like my client Mark. When I asked him why he thought she was cheating, he said he had a gut feeling. Nothing more, nothing less. Imagine if he did not listen. Okay, as promised, here is the rest of the story.

First, a quick note. The bride was from a prominent family, and 500-plus friends had gathered that day to hear her vow, "In sickness and in health... till death do us part." I just hoped that the death part wouldn't happen during the salad course.

"Lovely," said the guests after both said, "I do." Then, it was off to the lavish hotel reception, where the groom decided to break with tradition and give the first toast. Mark looked handsome and determined as he raised a crystal glass.

"I want to thank my beautiful wife, Melissa," he said. "And here's to my amazing best man, Tim. In fact, I have a giant surprise for both of you."

On cue, the lights dimmed and a video began to play on a large screen. There were Melissa moaning and Jeff groaning, each one hundred percent lacking in clothing, as they did things in a Mustang convertible that belonged in the *Kama Sutra*. (You had to give it to Melissa—she was pretty flexible. Note to self: Take a yoga class.)

Amid gasps of horror, Mark concluded his wedding screening with these words: "I had the video uploaded for all of our guests. You can find it taped to the bottom of your seat. Take it home for your viewing pleasure."

"Good night," he said.

And then he dropped the mic.

At that point, half of the men in the room began to beat the crap out of the best man while many of the bride's family took aim at Mark. The last part is why he wanted my guys on hand, since many are former police officers. He needed a beefy escort out of Dodge, which we provided.

"I knew she was cheating, but I needed closure," Mark said as we raced him out of the room.

"Everybody needs closure," I said, "just not that much.

I became a private investigator for reasons beyond closure. I've been referred to often as a natural healer, and I thrive on helping people get to the other side of whatever side of what they are going through that might be difficult in their life. Whether it's personal or professional, I have witnessed struggles the average person could not even imagine.

So when I talk about trusting your gut, I'm talking about women's intuition, spidey sense, gut feelings—that moment when something just physically doesn't feel right. When I talk about manifestation, I always ask people to tap into what they're feeling *physically*.

In my work, hindsight shows up a lot. As a PI, I can tell you: almost every single client has said something like:

"I wish I'd listened… before I got married."

"I knew, six months in, six years in, something was off."

They saw the patterns. They felt the signs. Their gut told them to pay attention. Clients would call and say, "I feel really stupid calling you, but something just doesn't feel right."

And I stop them right there: "No. If you have a feeling, be curious. Explore it. Whether you hire us, hire someone else, or look into it yourself, don't ignore it."

Maybe it's not infidelity. Maybe it's a shopping addiction. A midlife crisis. Financial secrets. It could be anything. But if your body is setting off sirens, you need to listen.

You can absolutely use your inner awareness as a tool. And science backs this up: Gut instinct is real.

Let's use relationships as an example. You get your heart broken into a million pieces, and you look back and think, *There were warning signs. I had a gut feeling. I couldn't explain it, but something felt off.*

I've seen it, time and time again. People in relationships do not realize that the person they're dating, living with, or even married to, is living a double life. Other families. Other partners. Other businesses. Just a completely different life than what they claimed. And they all say the same thing: "I had this feeling…"

So when you're on the floor, in a fetal position, at your lowest low, I want you to remember that feeling and never let it go. By that, I mean remember what it felt like to not listen to your gut. Remember the warning signs, the sirens, the gut punches, and don't brush them off next time.

Now, I'm not saying to walk away from people at the first red flag. I'm not saying not to give people chances. But what I am saying is be curious about *why* you're feeling what you're feeling. And if you've got doubts, questions, or concerns, investigate them. Mentally. Physically. Spiritually. Do not ignore it.

Check in with your instincts when it matters. Don't set them aside. Don't tell yourself, *It's just me being crazy*. Don't believe that voice that says, *My ex, my boss, my partner said I'm nuts, so I must be nuts*.

Here's the thing. So many of my clients over the last two decades have tried to pass off their intuition as anxiety. But I strongly encourage you to be curious.

In my opinion, anxiety is often your body's emergency alarm. It shows up when fear is triggered, whether there's proof or not. And it comes with physical symptoms: sweaty palms, flushed face, racing heart, shaky hands. If you're experiencing those things, absolutely go talk to someone. But for me—and for the thousands and thousands of people I've worked with—intuition feels different. It's not in your chest but in your gut. You go to bed thinking something feels off. You know something's not right. And it nags. And it lingers. And sometimes, it shouts.

It took me years of practice to understand how my body reacts when it's anxiety versus when it's instinct. Something on the inside will start reacting because something on the outside is off. That's how I've learned to separate the two.

Never, ever, minimize what you're feeling or how you're experiencing it. Before we had modern tech and research, we had instinct. Animals use it to thrive and survive. They sense danger before they see it. That's their gut. And it keeps them alive. So if it's part of your design, why wouldn't you use it?

You've probably been told to "trust your gut"—but no one tells you how. They make intuition sound like a mystical superpower, when really, it's the most practical and underused tool you have. It's your built-in truth detector. Your internal green light—or red flag. And here's the kicker: It's always been there. Most people just stopped listening to it. We override it with logic, drown it in noise, or silence it with self-doubt. But when you learn how to tune in, trust it, and lead with it? Everything changes. Here's what I know for sure about intuition—and why it's the most powerful advantage you already have.

- *Intuition is intelligence in real time.* It's not a hunch—it's your brain and body working together, reading patterns, energy, and experience faster than you can process consciously. When something feels off or undeniably right, pay attention. Your intuition already knows what your mind is still trying to figure out.
- *Your gut speaks before your mind has time to talk you out of it.* Logic protects. Intuition guides. One keeps you safe; the other moves you forward. Start listening to that first hit of knowing before fear or overthinking gets a vote.
- *Your body never lies.* Tightness. Lightness. Pressure. Ease. Physical cues are often the first sign your inner compass is signaling yes or no. Instead of brushing it off, start checking in. Your body will always tell the truth—even when your mind won't.
- *Noise drowns out knowing.* When you're constantly scrolling, comparing, or crowdsourcing decisions, your inner voice gets buried under everyone else's opinions. Creating space—silence, solitude, stillness—isn't a luxury. It's a strategy.
- *Intuition is not emotion—it's instinct.* Emotions can be loud, fast, and reactive. Intuition is calm, clear, and steady. The difference? Intuition doesn't panic. It just knows.

- *Self-trust is built one intuitive decision at a time.* The more you act on your gut, the stronger it gets. Even small decisions made from inner knowing start to rebuild the kind of trust that can't be shaken.

When you lead with intuition, personally and professionally, you gain a massive edge because most people are still ignoring the signs right in front of them.

But life is persistent. First, it taps you on the shoulder. If you don't listen, it taps harder. Eventually, if you keep ignoring it, it hits you with a brick wall. And that's when people say, "I knew. I had a feeling. I just didn't listen."

So stop ignoring your body. Stop silencing your gut. Why would you hide your superpower?

That inner voice? It's not a whisper—it's a knowing. And deep down, *you've always known.* Even when you ignored it. Even when you talked yourself out of it. Your gut has never lied to you. It's the part of you that doesn't need proof, just trust. It speaks through stillness, discomfort, chills, and sparks. And the moment you start honoring it over the noise, you begin leading from your truth, not your fear. You don't need to earn that voice or justify it. You just need to stop abandoning it. Because self-trust isn't something you build when it's convenient—it's something you commit to when it matters most.

And trust me, it always matters.

ROCKSTAR RECAP

Your intuition is not soft. It is sharp. Your gut is your built-in truth detector. And it's been trying to keep you safe all along the way.

Journal Prompts For Readers

- ★ What's one moment where your gut was right, and you ignored it?

_____
_____
_____
_____

- ★ How does intuition show up in your body?

_____
_____
_____
_____

- ★ How do you distinguish between instinct and anxiety?

_____
_____
_____
_____

Make Your Move
Start a seven-day journal. Each day, jot down one moment where you trusted or questioned your instincts.

CHAPTER EIGHT
COMFORTABLE BEING UNCOMFORTABLE

"You can choose courage, or you can choose comfort. You cannot have both."
~ Brené Brown

"Get comfortable being uncomfortable" isn't just a quote—it's a way of life for me. You can have courage or comfort, but never both. So powerful. Say it again! Growth lives in the stretch, the risk, the moment your voice shakes, but you speak anyway. Choosing courage means betting on yourself when the outcome isn't guaranteed and doing it over and over again until it is. Comfort keeps you safe. Courage makes you a legend.

One of the biggest breakthroughs I had in therapy was realizing exactly that—I can do hard things.

In the thick of it, when everything feels impossible, you learn by doing. You realize that discomfort is the only path through hard things. You can't avoid it. You can't go around it. You have to move through it. And by that, I mean run at it. Break through it like a wrecking ball. Deke it out and race around it. Army crawl if you have to. It doesn't matter how you do it—just get to the other side, whatever that looks like for you.

Change isn't comfortable. The deeper I dove into private investigation, the more uncomfortable I became with the walls I'd built around myself. It wasn't that I didn't love solving mysteries—I did. But something was shifting. I was doing more than solving problems. I was helping people in crisis. People who were hurting, vulnerable, unsure of where to turn next. I realized that it wasn't just about what was on the outside. It was about what was happening within. Within them and within me.

That's when I got serious about life coaching. I looked everywhere in my own industry for mentorship. Doors slammed in my face. I was laughed at. Rejected. Sworn at. Now, I do want to give credit to one person, an ex-police detective, Tommy, who did offer some mentorship. But I needed more. I needed consistent guidance. Everyone does.

There's no paved highway when you're a founder or an entrepreneur. You figure it out as you go. Having a support system—people to bounce ideas off of, to talk through challenges—is powerful, regardless of whether or not they're in your industry, but I didn't know that at the time.

I thought I had to network inside the industry. And when that didn't work, and trust me, I asked everyone, I felt stuck. Then I found Tony Robbins.

Just like that, everything shifted. It wasn't about him being rude; it was about him challenging me. Pushing me beyond the limits I'd put on myself.

The truth was, I didn't want to get uncomfortable. I pushed back so hard that I delayed my own growth because of fear, ego, pride, or all of the above.

Eventually, I went back, I got certified, and we laughed about it later. But the lesson stuck: Growth only happens outside your comfort zone.

It doesn't happen when you're sitting in the safe zone, saying, "I'm good. I'll just keep doing what I'm doing." If you want to grow as a person, as a leader, as a professional, it's not going to be easy, and it won't be comfortable. Whether you're training for a marathon, becoming a doctor, or building a business, discomfort is part of the deal.

Think about little kids and growing pains—their bones, muscles, and ligaments literally ache as they stretch. It's no different for adults. You'll face failure, fear, and rejection. None of it feels good. But it's part of the process. It's the cost of evolving.

So if something in your life needs to change, change it. Don't let "comfortable" be your ceiling. You can trade a steady job for a life with more meaning. You can turn daily survival into personal fulfillment. When you start celebrating your wins with confidence, you'll find new threads of possibility.

Now, let me circle back. When Tony told me I was made for the big stage, I didn't believe him. Deep down, I think I always knew I loved it. But fear held me back. Fear of failing. Fear of falling. But who cares? I'm not about perfection—I'm about impact.

If you want to create impact, share your story, and teach through experience, you've got to step out of your comfort zone. It's scary, but it's also exciting. It's like the slow climb on a roller coaster. You hear the clicks, you know the drop is coming, and your mind spins with every worst-case scenario. But once you're flying down that track with the wind in your face—that's freedom.

The trick is to shift your mindset from fear to *excitement*. That's what happens when you reframe discomfort. Your world opens. Look at someone like David Goggins. That man shattered bones and ran marathons through the pain. I'm not saying you need to go full-on Navy SEAL, but he is such a legend.

When I want to do something that scares me, I become a little obsessed with the worst that could happen. Before I started speaking on stage, I asked myself, *What's the worst-case scenario?* I might trip. All the lights will go out. Maybe no one will laugh. Maybe they'll check their phones. And can I survive that? Absolutely.

That's how I work through fear. I don't avoid it; I walk right into it. As long as you're growing in healthy, aligned ways, go ahead and obsess. Let discomfort be your new normal, and let it drive you. Most people stop the moment they feel uncertain. But that's exactly when you need to keep going. Tell yourself, *I might not get the outcome I want, but I won't stay stuck. I'm not sitting here in my poopy diaper, feeling sorry for myself. I'm moving through it.* When you do that, your whole life changes.

I once heard a story that Elon Musk's wife had trained herself to treat discomfort as just another feeling, no different than nervousness, excitement, or anticipation—something to acknowledge rather than fear.

Growth never shows up in comfort. You already know that. But what no one tells you is that the most successful, confident, unshakable women you see? They're not fearless—they're fluent in discomfort. They've made a habit of doing the things most people avoid. The conversations. The risks. The reinvention. They've trained for it. Getting uncomfortable isn't a punishment—it's a portal. It's where your next level lives. But most people never get there... because the second it feels hard, they retreat. So let's flip the script. Here's what I've learned about why discomfort is non-negotiable—and how to rise through it instead of running from it.

- *You keep waiting to feel ready before you make a move* You tell yourself you'll start when you're more confident, more qualified, more "together." But readiness is a delay disguised as a goal. The truth? You create readiness by moving. Every rockstar I know started before they felt ready—and they became unstoppable by doing it scared, not safe.

- *You're afraid of judgment, so you play it safe* You tone yourself down so no one has an opinion, but they will anyway. Playing small doesn't protect you from criticism; it only ensures you never feel fully seen. The ones who rise are the ones who let themselves be fully expressed, not universally accepted.
- *You avoid hard conversations to keep the peace* Let's be real: keeping quiet doesn't preserve peace—it just buries your power. When you avoid the hard conversations, you abandon your own needs. Speaking up with clarity and courage isn't conflict—it's self-respect. And the more you do it, the more you build trust in your voice.
- *You stay stuck in what's familiar because you know how to survive it* Familiar isn't always safe—it's just known. Staying in survival mode might feel like control, but it's often just fear in disguise. Choosing discomfort on purpose—through change, growth, and risk—is how you move from surviving to actually living.
- *You delay decisions because you don't want to make the wrong one* Perfection paralysis is a confidence killer. The truth is, most clarity comes after the decision, not before. You don't need to see the whole path to take the next step. Choose, act, adjust. Leaders don't need certainty—they move with intention.
- *You quit when it starts to feel too hard* Discomfort doesn't mean you're off track—it often means you're right on it. Growth will stretch you, challenge you, and yes, sometimes exhaust you. But quitting too soon is how people stay the same. Resilience is built in the tension, not the easy wins.
- *You over-prepare to avoid vulnerability* If you think you can out-plan your way into feeling safe, you'll burn out trying. Over-preparing is often just fear wearing a productive mask. The truth? Confidence doesn't come from controlling every variable—it comes from trusting yourself when you can't.

- *You confuse discomfort with danger* Not every uncomfortable moment is a red flag. Sometimes it's a green light in disguise. The stretch, the nerves, the uncertainty? Those are signs you're expanding. Learn to sit with the edge of discomfort—because that's exactly where breakthroughs are born.

We are programmed to avoid fear, uncertainty, and challenge, but that's where the growth is. That's where the magic is. So check in with yourself. What are you trading in exchange for safety? Freedom often lives *just past* that fear.

Humans are incredible at surviving. In my career, I've seen people survive betrayal, heartbreak, trauma, and loss and rebuild lives they never thought possible. In the thick of it, they couldn't see a way forward, but on the other side, there was beauty, strength, and freedom.

The truth is, nothing epic ever comes from playing it safe. Get comfortable being uncomfortable because that's where your growth lives. In the stretch. In the silence before the leap. In the moments your voice shakes, but you speak anyway. Comfort might keep you safe, but courage is what makes you a legend.

ROCKSTAR RECAP

Growth lives just outside your comfort zone. Get comfortable with being uncomfortable.

Journal Prompts For Readers

★ What area of your life feels the most uncomfortable right now?

_____

_____

_____

_____

★ What story are you telling yourself about discomfort?

_____

_____

_____

_____

★ What might be waiting for you on the other side of discomfort?

_____

_____

_____

_____

Make Your Move
Do one thing today that stretches you emotionally, socially, or creatively, and reflect on the experience.

CHAPTER NINE
PERFECTLY IMPERFECT

"You are imperfect. You are wired for struggle,
but you are worthy of love and belonging."
~ Brené Brown

To me, perfectly imperfect means owning every flaw, scar, and detour like they're part of your backstage pass. You weren't built to be flawless. You were built to be *real, resilient,* and *on fire*. You were wired for the struggle, but you're worthy of the spotlight, the seat at the table, and the whole damn encore. Your imperfections aren't weaknesses—they're your *wildest superpower*.

Back in the day, I used to model. At one of the jobs, we were sent to the zoo for a shoot. Two male photographers were there, and from the moment I arrived, they made it clear I wasn't what they wanted. It wasn't just that they didn't like my look—they humiliated me. With gorillas in the background, they started in with the body-shaming. Told me I was too fat (I was 105 lbs) and said they couldn't believe someone like me was sent to them from my agency. One of them even said the gorillas were doing a better job than I was. It ended with, "Get the f**k off my set."

I didn't let them see me cry, but I was crushed. I started to question myself. *Was I fat? Was what he said about me true? Did I really suck at this modelling thing that was supposed to be fun?*

Sadly, those moments stay with you. And although you eventually get past it. I believe it takes a little piece from you every time if you let it. Until one day you wake up and you start to wonder: *Where did I learn to treat myself like this?* Because when you look at little kids running around with shirts above their belly buttons, various body shapes, but with pure joy on their faces, because they don't see or don't care about "imperfections." That shame comes later.

For most people, it starts somewhere between the ages of five and seven, when someone makes fun of them, usually more than once. That's when the outside voices begin to shape how we see and feel about ourselves. I was bullied for how I looked, and it stuck. But not just from the photographers, for years before I started to model.

I know this is one of the many driving forces behind mentorship and helping others. Especially younger girls. Because if I could talk to younger me, I would tell her to shut out the outside influences. It's just noise.

I believe this is one of the biggest reasons I'm writing this book. It starts young, especially for girls. We have to teach them self-belief early: *You are enough,* just as you are.

In the modeling world, especially in the mid-'80s and '90s, thin was in. I could show you pictures where my bones were literally sticking out. I was on starvation diets, wasting away—and still, I was called fat. It's absurd, but at the time, because I heard it continuously, I started to believe it. That belief led me to a point in my adult life where I removed all the full-length mirrors from my house.

At first, it was supposed to be temporary. But the freedom I felt was unreal. I didn't have to beat myself up every time I walked out the door. It wasn't the photographer's fault anymore—it was me. I had let their voices become mine. Every time I looked in the mirror, I used to point out my muffin top, stretch marks, and everything I disliked. I would speak to myself in ways I'd never speak to anyone else.

That's when I knew I had to stop. Through my work with Tony Robbins and the mindset work I dove into, I realized our internal dialogue is everything. The story you tell yourself becomes the life you live. So I got rid of the mirrors. I kept only one small one and the bathroom mirror. And you know what? I was so much happier and kinder to myself.

I started seeing my stretch marks as warrior wounds. I created *life,* four times. That's not a flaw—that's a superpower. I stopped comparing myself to the airbrushed, Photoshopped standards that were never real to begin with. I accepted every part of me—the flaws, the scars, the things society tells us to fix. I finally gave myself grace. And there's such power and peace in that.

When I coach clients, I hand them a Sharpie and a sticky note. They laugh and say, "This is the smallest journal I've ever seen!" and I tell them, "Yeah, and it's about to change everything."

I'd have them watch a quick video called "Why Do We Fall," then for thirty days, they'd write a simple affirmation on a sticky note starting with "I am." *I am strong. I am enough. I am bold.* Then they'd stick it on their mirror to read in the morning and at night. That little routine rewired their self-talk. It worked every time. Every single one of them felt better afterward. It helped them look at their imperfections and, maybe for the first time, see them as parts of their power.

Eventually, the work moved from the physical to the emotional. Maybe your imperfections aren't something you see in the mirror—maybe they're moments you're not proud of. Times you hurt someone. Times you weren't your best self. There is power in facing those, too. Owning them. Saying, *That wasn't okay, but I'm better now. I've grown.*

Forgiving yourself is where real healing begins. It's the most freeing thing you can do. And when you start giving yourself that grace, that space to shift and reflect, everything starts to change.

This book isn't written from the finish line. I am still a work in progress. I feel that we can all be better every day. Sometimes I'm in the middle of the mess because life throws you a curveball. Still learning. Still rising. But if there's one thing I know for sure, it's that you don't rise because you've got it all figured out. You rise because you stop hiding who you really are. *Perfectly imperfect* means I've owned every scar, every detour, every moment that tried to break me, and I turned them into my fuel. I wasn't built to be flawless. I was built to be *real, resilient,* and *unapologetically bold.*

So were you. I didn't rise because it was easy. I rose because staying down was never an option. And now it's your turn.

Say yes to the version of you that's always been waiting to take the stage. The struggle is not a detour—it's the training ground.

I had big dreams. And not just soft, subtle dreams—I'm talking *empire-building, soul-defining, wildly ambitious* dreams.

And for six years, I didn't have a mirror in the house. Not because I didn't care, but because I was afraid of who I might see. I was simply exhausted by the habit of judging myself unkindly. Removing the mirror made it easier. It was that simple.

I knew it wouldn't be forever, and I definitely didn't think it would last that long. I believe I was too busy mending the wounds and learning to be kind to myself to even notice it was gone. It was a relief.

And here's the kicker—what I learned when I finally faced her: that reflection wasn't a failure. She was a fighter. A survivor. A rockstar in the rawest sense.

Three easy actions with massive impact when you start owning your story:

✔ Knowing your story helps you stop second-guessing who you are and start making aligned, confident decisions.
You lead from clarity instead of constantly chasing validation.

✔ Knowing your story turns your past into purpose.
What once felt heavy becomes fuel, and people connect with the real you, not the filtered version.

✔ Knowing your story lets you rewrite what it means to rise.
You stop hiding the hard parts and start using them as proof that you're already built for more.

We spend so much of our lives trying to outgrow our imperfections—like they're flaws we're supposed to hide or fix. But the truth is, the most magnetic, powerful, and unforgettable women I know are the ones who show up as they are, not as they think they "should" be. Perfection isn't what makes you powerful—presence does. Realness does. The willingness to lead from your truth, even when it's messy, even when it's raw, especially when it's vulnerable. That's where trust is built. That's where confidence is born.

Being perfectly imperfect means you stop apologizing for the chapters that shaped you. You wear your experiences, your heartbreak, your grit, your rise, not like baggage, but like a badge of honor. When you stop trying to edit yourself for approval, you give others permission to meet the real you—and more importantly, you give yourself permission to finally breathe. This isn't about being careless. It's about being clear. When you know who you are, what you've walked through, and how far you've come, you don't need to prove your worth—you embody it.

So here's your reminder: You weren't built to be flawless. You were built to be whole. Want to start showing up that way? Write the version of your story you've been scared to own—and read it back without judgment. Look in the mirror and say one thing you admire about the woman staring back. Catch yourself in a moment of self-doubt, and choose compassion over critique. These are small moves, but they build big power. Because when you can love yourself exactly as you are, you become unstoppable. Perfectly imperfect, and powerful as hell.

Resilience isn't about walking around unscathed—it's about showing up with your scars *and still owning the room*. It's about being *perfectly imperfect* and letting that truth become your power.

See Yourself Clearly

Don't just pass by the mirror. *Stand there*. Look long enough to recognize the warrior behind your eyes. Too many of us avoid our own reflection, not because we're vain, but because we're afraid of what's staring back. But here's the truth: you can't build confidence if you refuse to see yourself.

Seeing yourself clearly means acknowledging everything you've lived through, without shame. The heartbreaks, the mistakes, the pivots, the comebacks. That reflection is not your past—it's your proof. It's the face of someone who didn't quit. Who kept moving. Who keeps *becoming*.

When you finally look and say, "Damn… I'm still standing," that's when real confidence begins.

Embrace the Messiness

Let go of the lie that things have to be tidy to be beautiful. The magic isn't in the perfect plan. It's in the wild detour, the storm you didn't see coming, and the way you found your footing in the middle of it.

Mess is the evidence of movement. It's proof that you're in the arena, not sitting on the sidelines.

Embracing the mess means making peace with your humanity. It's knowing that you don't need to clean yourself up to be powerful. You don't need to "fix" who you are to take the mic or walk into the boardroom.

Your story isn't powerful because it's flawless. It's powerful because you *survived the fallout* and kept rising anyway.

Lead with Your Heart

The mind will try to keep you safe. It will whisper doubts and calculate risks and cling to logic. But your heart? Your heart is the battlefield general. It remembers every fall, every climb, every quiet win no one else saw.

Leading with your heart means letting your *feelings* be part of the process, not something you apologize for. It means trusting that your inner wisdom is valid, even when it's not easy to explain. It's knowing that being soft doesn't make you weak, and being emotional doesn't make you irrational. It makes you *human*.

And when you lead with your heart *and* your head, you become unstoppable. Because now you're not just performing—you're connected. Rooted. Unshakable.

Find Beauty in the Chaos

The most powerful transformations don't happen when things are calm. They happen in the storm. That's where your mettle is tested. That's where the old version of you dies, so the next one can rise.

Chaos doesn't mean failure. It means something is shifting. It means growth is breaking through the surface. The dream is rearranging itself. So don't run from the chaos—study it. Listen to it. Let it shape you.

You don't have to have it all figured out. You just have to keep showing up in the middle of the mess with open hands and an open heart. That's where the most breathtaking breakthroughs are born.

Own Your Story

Your story is your superpower. Not the polished version you post online—the real one. The one that's still in process. The one that holds both power and pain. When you own your story, *all of it*, you stop hiding. You stop apologizing. You stop trying to edit yourself to fit into rooms you were born to lead.

You are not here to be digestible. You are here to be undeniable. That means telling the truth about who you are, where you've been, and what you've overcome, without waiting for permission. Because once you own your story, nobody else gets to rewrite it for you.

Be Grateful for Your Scars

Scars are sacred. They're evidence that the wound has healed. That you walked through fire and lived to tell the tale. That something tried to break you, and it didn't win.

Your scars aren't ugly. They're *honors*. They're the receipts for every time you didn't give up. They are your timeline of resilience, etched right onto your body and your soul.

And you know what? Some people won't understand them. That's okay. Your scars weren't made to impress; they were made to *remind you who you are*.

Wear them like armor. Speak of them with pride. Let them fuel your mission, your fire, and your fight.

Let's get one thing straight: *Perfect isn't the goal. Real is.*

Because real women, ones who fall, cry, curse, fight, rise, and still find a way to smile at the sunrise, they're the ones changing the world. Not because they've mastered perfection, but because they *refused to stay small in the face of imperfection.*

So here's the invitation:

Stop shrinking. Stop editing. Stop waiting to be flawless before you step into the light.

The truth is, no one ever changed the world by being flawless.

We rise because we've fallen.

We speak the truth because we've been silenced.

We stand tall because we've been brought to our knees—and got back up *anyway*.

Here's the unfiltered reality:

You're not here to be perfect. You're here to be *real*. You're here to be *resilient*. And real women, resilient, messy, relentless women, are rewriting the rules, one imperfect step at a time.

You're not made of glass.

You're made of grit.

And if you're still standing, still dreaming, still daring to show up with your whole story?

You've already won.

Because being *perfectly imperfect* isn't a weakness—it's your *wildest advantage*.

And confidence? That's not something you wait for.

It's something you *own*. Flaws, scars, stretch marks, stumbles—*all of it*.

That's Rockstar Confidence.

And it's yours now.

ROCKSTAR RECAP

Imperfection isn't your flaw. It's your fingerprint. The moment you accept your full self, physically, mentally, emotionally, and spiritually, is the moment you unlock your true power. You were built to be bold, resilient, and unapologetically you.

Journal Prompts For Readers

★ What do you still criticize in yourself that others admire?

_____

_____

_____

_____

★ What was your earliest belief about what made someone good enough?

_____

_____

_____

_____

★ What are your imperfections teaching you about grace?

_____

_____

_____

_____

Make Your Move
Look in the mirror and admit three things about yourself that you've judged. Follow each with, "... *and I love you anyway.*"

CHAPTER TEN
FROM TRAUMA TO PURPOSE

*"Do not judge me by my success. Judge me by how many times
I fell down and got back up again."*
~ Nelson Mandela

This chapter, "From Trauma to Purpose," isn't about the fall—it's about the choice to rise, over and over, even when no one's clapping. It's about quiet courage, private battles, and the kind of strength that doesn't need a spotlight to be real. I don't measure success the same way others do. I measure it by every moment we show up anyway. This is what it means to rise with purpose and lead like a Rockstar.

There's something people don't talk about enough—the choice to rise. Not once. Not twice. But every damn time life knocks you flat. I've been through it. Trauma tried to take me out. Grief, betrayal, heartbreak, self-doubt—it all came swinging. And I won't lie, it hit hard. But I hit back harder. Not with noise. Not with ego. With *resilience*. With fire. With the decision to stand up every time the world thought I'd stay down.

Confidence isn't born—it's built. Built in the messy middle. Built when no one's clapping. Built when you're crying in your car and still show up like a legend.

There's no straight line to purpose. There's falling. There's rebuilding. There's figuring it out with shaky hands and a steady heart. I didn't just "find" purpose—I *earned* it. By choosing not to let trauma define me. By turning pain into fuel. By showing up for myself over and over again until the belief caught up.

My power didn't come from perfection. It came from the rise.

My confidence wasn't handed to me. I became it.

My purpose was never lost—it was waiting for me on the other side of the comeback.

So no, this chapter isn't about falling. It's about *owning* the fact that I got back up. That I *chose* to become the woman I am. That every crack in my story is exactly where the light got in.

I don't shrink. I rise.

I don't break. I rebuild.

I don't apologize for who I had to become to survive—she's the reason I lead like a powerhouse now.

If you're reading this, wondering if it gets better, yes.

If you're waiting to feel "ready," you already are.

If you think the struggle disqualifies you from greatness, it doesn't.

It qualifies you. It makes you the story.

You're not behind. You're not broken. You're becoming.

And trust me, when you meet your purpose face to face, it'll all make sense.

This is the rise.

This is the fire.

When we recognize we are in control of owning our shift, we allow ourselves to be vulnerable and empower ourselves through the truth. It is at this key moment that we can change our internal narrative that we tell ourselves about an experience.

I've had to rewrite the narrative many times in my own life. When I was twenty-one years old, I worked as a bartender at three different bars in town. I had just moved out on my own and was determined.

At that time, I began to date someone who ended up not being a very good person. I was modeling part-time and booked an important gig in Europe. My parents had a party for me, and the boyfriend was there. I guess he didn't believe I'd leave him, even for a short period of time, and he was quite upset.

"I'm leaving in the morning," I told him.

"No, you're not," he said.

On the way home, he drove off a large, cliff-like hill in an attempt to Thelma and Louise us! Obviously not a smart move for me to get in the car with him when he was so upset. My head went through the windshield, and I vaguely remember an ambulance arriving. My boyfriend grabbed me, and through the glare of sirens and the rivers of blood, he whispered, "You don't tell anyone what really happened, or you'll regret it." Then, he pretended to pass out.

Since he pretended to be unconscious, the ambulance took him away first. I told my friends what really happened, and they were pissed. My dad and mom were devastated. At the time, I was totally embarrassed that I let this happen to me. Little did I know, it would give me PI insight later when dealing with victims of abuse. I still have a massive scar on the back of my head to remind me of where I had been.

My Hungarian, very European parents taught me to work hard, and I did. In fact, my father and I had always talked about opening a restaurant together, once I was released from the hospital. He knew I was looking for something more and knew I had the entrepreneurial spirit. He told me that once he returned from his trip to Hungary, he would open our restaurant. But that was a dream for a different lifetime.

On the morning of his return, while I was restocking the bar, I had a feeling in my gut. I was so distracted by this uneasy feeling that I actually slipped off a beer keg and fell flat on my back in the freezer. Looking back, it was quite funny, but at the time, I was terrified, thinking it would be a very long time before anyone found me.

It turned out I had just knocked the wind out of myself, and aside from a sore back, I was fine. I was supposed to pick up Dad from the airport that evening, and I just couldn't shake the feeling that something was off.

My beloved dad passed away when I was twenty-one and living in my own apartment. My father decided to go to Hungary for a visit. He could see that I had the spirit to open my own business but wasn't passionate about fashion anymore.

"Honey, when I get back, we'll open our own business together. A restaurant," he promised.

It wasn't meant to be in this lifetime. The day he was supposed to come home, I was working at one of the bars, counting beers in the beer fridge. It was 10:30 in the morning in Canada, and I was due to pick him up at the airport that evening but had this pit in my gut. It was a physical feeling that wouldn't go away. I had to get on top of a four-foot keg. All of a sudden, I was on the floor with the wind knocked out of me.

I couldn't catch my breath. My racing mind screamed, *If no one comes, you will die here. Alone!*

Somehow, I caught my breath and got back up. A full bar of thirty people was waiting for me. Meanwhile, my sister called to say that Dad's plane was coming in at 8:30 p.m.

She called again before I left for the airport.

"I'm leaving here soon to go pick up Dad," I said in a rush.

On the other end of the line, she was bawling.

"Dad. It's Dad. He's dead. Dad died," she said. "They had a big going-away party for him in Hungary. I don't know what happened, but he had a massive stroke in the shower before going to the airport. There was nobody there, and he basically drowned."

I couldn't process the news. *Dad didn't get on the plane. Dad was hurt. No one came. Dad died. He was alone? I was supposed to be on that trip with him.*

It was true that he had a few minor attacks, mini-strokes, in the past, but doctors cleared him to fly despite the idea that he needed a triple bypass immediately.

"I'm fine," Dad insisted. "When I get back, I will really look after my health, and we will open that business together."

Bleak times followed, including dealing with my grief-stricken mother. I knew I would never see my dad again. He would never meet my children, which was so sad to me. Although I was his little girl, I knew he wanted a boy more than anything in the world. I had four who would never be able to hug him, kiss him, build things with him, or know his incredible, funny sense of humor.

Granny had that European, old-school mentality that as a woman you needed to carry on the name and legacy by having a boy. It was a European way of thinking. Boys were the prize, and girls were nice. My father not having a son but raising me to have the same independence as a son proved to be his legacy. I believe he is proud of me.

This was probably why I kept my last name and gave my father's first and last name to all of my children.

Dad was a very powerful force in my life. I found my true passion when I opened up my own private investigation agency. My father would have been in the thick of things and definitely would have wanted a badge and a gun (lol).

I believe that somewhere in the universe, he knows my boys and loves the business. He even probably has that shiny badge pinned to his chest

For a long time, it played over and over in my head. *He suffered a stroke in the shower, and because no one was there, he drowned. He was getting ready to go to the airport. No one was there, and he died alone.* I felt so much guilt and sorrow. My hero and mentor was gone. That day, my life as I knew it changed forever.

My father would never get to meet any of my future children, to be a grandfather, to walk me down the aisle, to grow old and continue to bug the shit out of me, as he did often. I was heartbroken. He was such a powerful force in my life. He always believed in me and encouraged me to follow my dreams, regardless of obstacles—I credit him for teaching me strength, love, and independence. I later learned that his time of death was the exact time I fell off the keg. Coincidence? I think not.

After his death, I was left wondering how to move forward. I was left to work through trauma and grief. I had never lived a day on this earth without him here, and doing so without him seemed impossible.

I had to make a choice: I had to choose to move forward. The experience gave me a new appreciation for life. It taught me how to live in the moment. And eventually, *I owned the shift*. I owned the new course my life had taken. I chose not to become a casualty of my tragedy.

If we believe in ourselves and have confidence that we are going to be okay, then it will be. I don't believe that we break—I believe that we bend. And if we do it with intent, we will be more flexible to experiences because of it. Our tragedies can hold us back or propel us forward, but they do not define us to our core. What *does* is how we pick ourselves back up after tragedy.

Death is not new to me, but my dad's was especially significant. Somebody had to go and pick up his body. Ultimately, it was my mother. My aunt and I made the decision, and though it was the hardest ask, we believed she needed that moment.

One thing I don't share often—because I'm so damn proud of who my mother is as a woman—is that she drank when I was younger. A lot. It was how they survived things in their world—escaping the

Hungarian Revolution, building a life out of rubble. But it made for a complicated upbringing. By the time my father died, she had been sober for two years. I was so proud of her.

When it came time for her to fly to retrieve his body, my sister took her to the airport. What I didn't know until much later was that she gave our mother a few shots before putting her on that plane. Maybe she thought it would calm her nerves. But when they came back, I saw that my mom had started drinking again. And just like that, I had a whole new layer of grief to carry. I dove into the 12 Steps (the guiding principles originally developed by Alcoholics Anonymous). I went with her to meetings. I supported her. But I was also angry, so angry, because I needed my mother, and instead of being allowed the time and space to grieve, I was back to caretaking.

My sister Cathi, meanwhile, moved to Vancouver, leaving me to hold everything together with Mom. We continuously tried to rebuild our relationship, but from that moment on, things between us were strained. She also drank quite a bit. But it wasn't just the drinking or the absence—it was all the little betrayals that added up. It was painful, especially since she was the only sibling I had. Our father was gone, and our extended family was small and aging. We were all we had.

Death changes people. My parents never taught us that death is just part of life. I've tried to do the opposite with my kids. I joke with them, not because it's funny, but because humor is sometimes the only way to hold yourself together. I say, "Nobody's getting out of here alive." Whether you believe in heaven, the universe, or something else entirely, I believe there's something beyond this life. That belief has been shaped by too many losses to count.

Cathi and I loved each other, but we struggled. My marriage, my children, and my life choices became friction points. We were very different. I accepted that, and she criticized my choices. She lived far away, and for years, she felt very absent.

Meanwhile, I was the one holding our mother up when she didn't show up. I was the one patching the cracks, carrying the weight. I was angry, and I carried that anger quietly for a long time.

Cathi was always the life of the party—six-foot-three, blonde, beautiful, wild, fun. She started Lollapalooza in Vancouver, moved to Los Angeles to chase her dreams in the music industry, and worked for Sony before starting her own label. On the outside, she was killing it. But she was also deeply troubled. She drank heavily, lived fast, and never admitted to the grip that addiction had on her. I had to accept that we lived very different lives. Not better or worse—just different.

Our moral compasses pointed in different directions. But we decided to try, for our mother and for each other. I brought her to Toronto. At the time, she had a boyfriend that I liked, Jerry. Things felt hopeful.

In 2018, my four boys, my mom, Matt, and I decided to go on a beach vacation. The night we got there, I kept seeing my phone light up. Jerry kept calling. I didn't think much of it—people butt-dial me all the time, especially with a name like Adrianne at the top of their contact list. But it wasn't a mistake. Jerry was sobbing. Cathi was gone.

Dead.

I couldn't process it. I thought it was a sick joke. But it was real. From what I was told, she had been out on St. Patrick's Day, partying. The next morning, no one could reach her. Jerry found her after her dog began barking outside her door. She had taken a bath after a long night and drowned. And yes, if you're wondering, water seems to be a recurring tragedy in my life. I joke about it sometimes because if I don't, I'll cry.

That call changed me. Losing someone young, vibrant, and full of life does that. She was only fifty-three. Gone in a breath. I had to tell my mom, who was in the next room with my kids. I had to tell my children. My one son began panicking so badly that we had to call a doctor—we thought he might be having a heart attack. The grief was so raw, so sudden, so massive. I tried to hold it together, like I always do. I've had to deliver that kind of news far too many times.

But something shifted. One of my sons, who had been struggling with mental health, said to me that night I will never forget, "I never want to see you and Grandma go through something like this again."

In that moment of excruciating sorrow, I felt an overwhelming amount of gratitude, love, and guilt.

Gratitude for my son's awakening. Love for the higher power that helped him get there. Guilt that I felt these emotions during such a traumatic time. To be honest, I felt that moment saved him in many ways. He started training every day, lost more than one hundred pounds, and started playing junior hockey. He seemed to have found purpose again. He got a tattoo of Cathi's death date and called it his "rebirth day." And while no life should have to end for another to begin, in many ways, I believe that loss gave him life again.

When Cathi passed, I had to send a distant family friend to clear out her things in Los Angeles. They brought back a few items, but most of it was lost. What stayed with me most wasn't what they found, but what they didn't. Her fridge was empty, save for a tenth of a bottle of vodka. Her cupboards were empty. She had built a life that was fun on the surface but incredibly lonely underneath. She never married, never had kids. And yet, I had a full house. A full life. People who needed me. Loved me. I had to find a way to honor her. And I did, in every way I could.

Grief and death affect everyone differently. I made a decision to lead from my wounds and turn them into wisdom. That's what loss can do. It may never make sense, but it can become a legacy.

This year was our first year owning The Streetsville Derbys™ Junior Hockey Club. My second son's dream was to own this team, as it is deeply rooted in the rich hockey tradition of Streetsville. Our mission is to foster connections, promote inclusivity, and make a lasting impact both on and off the ice. The Derbys are part of the Provincial Junior Hockey League (PJHL), the world's largest junior hockey league, sanctioned by Hockey Canada. This historic team, founded in 1967, represents more than just competition; it embodies community spirit and the pursuit of excellence.

Our summit had just ended, and two days later, we learned that one of our players had died. He had scored the winning playoff goal. He had dreams, an incredible family, friends, and teammates who loved him. And then—he was gone.

The grief that hit those young men was unlike anything I'd ever seen. We cried. We held space. And we made sure his life would continue to matter.

We created a scholarship in his name: *The Streetsville Derbys Junior Hockey Club Scholarship*, in memory of Gary Grant Jr., a fund that helps other athletes pursue education, skilled trades, or continue their hockey careers.

For me, during loss, when we lead from purpose and love, we build meaning. We find purpose in the pain. We turn tragedy into transformation.

That's why I share stories like this. You don't know who needs to hear it, whose life you might save. After Cathi died, I changed how I lived, what I gave attention to, and how I worked. I knew I had a different purpose I needed to pursue. I saw the gap in support for women, especially in the chaos, the middle owning their shift, or during a transitional time in their lives.

As a female entrepreneur, mother, and trailblazer, I'd felt it myself. I want to create a space for women to rise as a person and a professional. That's when *I Am Unbreakable* was born. My mission is to amplify opportunity, funding, and the remarkable voices that drive social impact, create legacies, and foster belonging. My goal is to empower one billion women before I leave this earth.

I want other women to know that their story matters. That they matter. That no matter their past or present, they are part of something bigger. So I created a Front-Row Sister community that is more than just a brand; we're a tribe of trailblazers, risk-takers, and legacy builders. We come together to support each other, share our stories, and lift as we rise. It's about creating a thriving ecosystem where women are championed to achieve their boldest ambitions. This isn't just about showing up; it's about standing out, owning your space, and pushing the boundaries of what's possible. Together, we create a sustainable foundation for growth, driving impact that reaches far beyond ourselves and ripples into our communities.

At I Am Unbreakable, collaboration is not just a concept; it's a catalyst for change. By uniting women entrepreneurs, founders, and leaders, we create a powerful ecosystem that amplifies voices, shares resources, and opens doors to new opportunities. This collective approach fosters resilience, drives innovation, and accelerates growth for women-led ventures.

Through strategic partnerships and shared experiences, our community challenges the status quo, addresses funding disparities, and paves the way for equitable access to capital and mentorship. By working together, we not only elevate individual success but also contribute to a more inclusive and thriving business landscape.

Collaboration at I Am Unbreakable means building a legacy where women support women, ensuring that the path to leadership and entrepreneurship is accessible, sustainable, and impactful for all.

This is how I chose to honor the trailblazers who shattered glass ceilings long before the phrase even existed. These impactful women forged paths with unyielding courage and determination, often overlooked in their time. It's time we shine a spotlight on their stories and recognize the extraordinary strength that has always been present in women.

History is filled with incredible women who stood tall against adversity, their achievements often hidden in the shadows. Yet, when we piece together their journeys, we discover a tapestry woven with resilience, innovation, and an unwavering belief in their potential.

Turning trauma into purpose doesn't mean romanticizing pain—it means refusing to let it be the end of your story. We don't rise because life was easy; we rise because we chose not to stay buried in what broke us. Your trauma may not be your fault, but your healing is your responsibility. And when you decide to take what tried to destroy you and turn it into something meaningful, you don't just change your life—you give others permission to do the same. Purpose isn't always found in a perfect plan. Sometimes, it's born in the wreckage—and rebuilt with intention.

> ✔ Shift from *Why did this happen to me?* to *What can I do with this now?*
> This one question transforms pain into power and keeps you in motion, not stuck in the past.

> ✔ Speak the truth you used to hide, even if it's just to yourself at first.
> When you stop carrying shame in silence, you start leading with substance. Your truth becomes your platform.

> ✔ Find one way to use your experience to serve someone else. It doesn't have to be loud—it just has to be real. Purpose multiplies when it moves beyond you

You can turn your pain into purpose. This is how we heal. This is how we honor the ones we've lost—by rising, and by helping others rise too.

ROCKSTAR RECAP

Your pain doesn't disqualify you. It depends; it deepens your impact. When you lead from your wounds, turn wisdom, your life becomes a legacy.

Journal Prompts For Readers

★ What grief have you not given language to?

_____

_____

_____

_____

★ How can you honor someone you've lost through how you live?

_____

_____

_____

_____

★ What is one way you've already turned pain into purpose?

_____

_____

_____

_____

Make Your Move
Reach out to someone who's grieving and offer your presence, not just your words.

CHAPTER ELEVEN
THE POWER OF I AM

"I know for sure what we dwell on is who we become."
~ Oprah Winfrey

"The Power of *I Am*" is the moment everything shifts. It's not a mantra—it's a declaration. It's what happens when you stop playing it safe, stop asking for permission, and start betting on yourself with everything you've got. Saying *I am* means owning your voice, your vision, your experiences, and your worth—no matter who doubts it. It's brave. It's bold. And it's the difference between staying stuck and becoming unbreakable.

As I started speaking to more and more women about the lives they imagined for themselves, I learned just how powerful our imaginations are. We become what we tell ourselves we are.

If a beautiful woman thinks, *I am ugly. I am overweight,* she becomes that person to herself, and that thought pattern is hard to shift. Instead, we have to tell ourselves new things. We have to describe our best qualities out loud: "I am love. I am caring. I am kind. I am a mother. I am a founder. I am unbreakable."

I Am Unbreakable was born from the women I served within the private investigation sector. These were women who were founders, entrepreneurs, CEOs, C-suites are just smashing it and crushing goals in their lives. Everything from multi-billion dollar corporations they'd built from the ground up to speaking on a stage with 200,000 people.

But the one commonality they all shared with me, in their very personal and intimate moments, as we filtered through whatever situation they needed my help with, and it was never a good one, was that they didn't feel a sense of belonging and confidence.

I remember when I started within the private investigation sector, I didn't belong. I was rejected by my peers. And I just knew that if I was feeling that way, so were so many other women.

These were women with big lives, lots of family, friends, coworkers, but there was still that *thing* stopping them from being authentic, from being vulnerable. It was a mask they had to wear, to be who people thought they should be versus who they truly, authentically were.

I so loved and enjoyed talking to people. I provided them a sense of belonging. So much so that I had people flying me out to Florida—"I need a couple of coaching sessions"—but it wasn't sustainable. It would have been a great life and career for me if I didn't have four young children, a husband, a mother... my own life. But I did want to affect women on a larger scale, so I decided to start the *I Am Unbreakable* podcast.

I started by interviewing guests and putting it out on YouTube, Spotify, Amazon, Apple, anywhere and everywhere. It became quite popular, quite quickly.

Then, I decided to start a magazine. At first, it was just going to be digital. But then we went into print. And I was able to land us in Chapters and Indigo before the magazine even turned a year old.

Every single person I spoke to loved the name *I Am Unbreakable*. It was always a conversation piece. People felt empowered just by saying it. And it just kept reiterating that the story we tell ourselves—the good one, the not-so-good one, and the one that's complete bullshit—is what we end up believing.

It's like that McDonald's commercial. When it first came out, you're like, okay, it's kind of catchy. Then you start singing, *"I'm lovin' it."* And by the fiftieth time you hear it, your brain just knows: *Oh, that's McDonald's. Big Mac. Golden Arches.* It's the same thing, and it's scientifically proven: If you attach a feeling or a thought to a word, that's what you become because that's what you believe.

There's so much power in saying the words "I am" followed by something kind and loving. And if you don't feel positive? Just say, "I am okay." You don't have to say, "I am unbreakable. I am fantastic." You can say, "I am love. I am loved. I am enough. I am worthy."

Funny how many years later, the Barbie movie came out, and it's all about "I am enough." And we are. We are all enough.

Demi Moore had a great speech when she accepted her award, her first in twenty-six years. She said something like, "If you continue to try to be enough for others, you'll always disappoint yourself." And the way she said it… it just hit.

A big part of what I teach is being okay with being enough for you, and based on your expectations. It doesn't mean 24/7 perfection. It means being whatever you can be in that moment, that day.

Of course, we all try to be the best version of ourselves that we can be. But always remember that there's so much power in knowing that you are okay, regardless of outside influences.

There are people I respect immensely who say the most important relationship you can foster is the one with yourself. So why do we give so much attention, love, and energy to our exterior relationships *before* we've built a healthy one with ourselves?

People look for power outside of themselves. They think it's the career, the family, the car, the money. But the power? It's in *you*. It's in statements like *I am*.

I believe in flipping the script. I tell anyone who will listen: "You are the writer, the director, the narrator, the actress/actor." You get to change what your inner voice says, just like I did when I talked about the mirror. You get to shape your reality.

How you speak to yourself is the most important thing you'll do in your life if you want any significant transformation or if you want to reach a goal. If you keep saying, *I'm so stupid. I'm such a loser. I can't believe I did that...*

Why not say: *Wow, I tried hard? Epic fail, waiting for the lesson? Time to pivot?*

I encourage you to rewrite and flip the script on any of those negative self-thoughts. By now, if you've gotten this far in the book, you already know I've asked you to speak out loud to yourself for thirty days and really focus on how you talk to yourself. Always ask: *Would I speak to another human being like that?* If the answer is no, my question is: *Why are you doing it to the most important person in your life—you?* If the answer is yes, there's another book for that, lol!

I often talk about rejection. I talk about rewording things. I look at people's pain points—relationships, careers, childhood trauma—and I suggest starting small. Pick one pain point a week. One a day. One a month. Whatever your comfort zone is. Then, start rewriting your script.

Write down words or actions that trigger you. It could be something as small as "Did you take out the garbage?" or someone honking and giving you the finger. It could be attached to rejection. Being cheated on. Left. Abandoned, and the list goes on.

Find those things that hurt your soul and try to flip them. Instead of abandonment? *New opportunity.* What's behind door number two?

There are different ways to do this. I'm not saying you need to do it *my* way. But do it *somehow*. Know that you *can* create change for yourself.

Thank you for your honesty—I hear you loud and clear.

You don't want drama. You want depth. You want something that's bold, real, stripped-down, and undeniably powerful. No hype. No theatrics. You want the reader to feel it in their chest and believe it's themselves you're speaking to.

The Power of I Am is the moment you stop waiting to become who you already are. It's not about becoming someone else. It's about coming home to the version of you who's always been there, before the noise, before the self-doubt, before the world taught you to shrink. "I am" is identity. It's authority. It's the foundation you build everything else on. When you say "I am," you're not making a wish; you're setting a standard. And from that moment on, how you move shifts. Because you're no longer asking for permission, you're acting like it already belongs to you.

You want your power back? Say it. Then live like you believe it.

"*I am* enough," not because everything is perfect, but because nothing has to be. Power doesn't come from performance. It comes from presence.

"*I am* the author of this story," even the hard chapters. No more hiding. No more skipping pages. This is yours to tell and yours to lead from.

"*I am* becoming the woman I needed," and I'm not turning back. Legacy doesn't wait for permission. It begins the moment you stop apologizing and start owning every part of your rise.

This is the Power of "I am."

Say it like your future depends on it, because it does.

I am. There is so much power in this simple phrase when used correctly. You are the person who defines and decides who you are.

You have the power to change your script.

You have the power to write a new story.

Because whoever you *believe* you are…

You will become.

ROCKSTAR RECAP

The stories you repeat about yourself shape your identity. So choose your new words and write your new life. Embrace the power of I am.

Journal Prompts For Readers

★ What are my statements?
_____
_____
_____
_____

★ What do you say or think that keeps you stuck?
_____
_____
_____
_____

★ What new identities are you ready to speak to exist?
_____
_____
_____
_____

★ Who do you become when you speak kindly to yourself?
_____
_____
_____
_____

Make Your Move
Write five *I am* statements that align with your future and say them out loud each morning this week.

CHAPTER TWELVE
YOU ARE A ROCKSTAR

"Love yourself first, and everything else falls into line."
~ Lucille Ball

Being a Rockstar isn't about fame, followers, or flashy titles. It's about *finally seeing yourself* the way you were always meant to be: powerful, bold, and legendary. It's loving yourself without conditions. Believing in yourself when no one's clapping. And choosing to back yourself like a legend, *especially* when it's hard. Being a Rockstar has nothing to do with a stage and everything to do with owning your story, standing in your truth, and refusing to play small.

- Confidence isn't born—it's built in chaos.
- Because the struggle is not a detour. It's the training ground.
- Rockstar Confidence isn't just a mindset—it's a movement. It's the fierce, unshakable energy that pulses through trailblazing women who are building empires, breaking rules, and redefining leadership on their own terms.

It's not about being the loudest in the room—it's about owning the damn room the moment you walk in. It's about showing up boldly in boardrooms, meetings, summits, and stages with a voice that doesn't ask for permission—it commands attention.

Rockstar Confidence is what fuels female founders who go first. The disruptors who build what's never been built. The women who launch brands from scratch, raise capital like legends, and pitch ideas that shake industries. These are the women who don't shrink to fit in—they expand to lead.

They don't just play the game—they rewrite the rules.

They don't just talk about impact—they become the impact.

This confidence doesn't come from waiting to be chosen. It's forged in fire. It's built through failure, discipline, audacity, and showing up every single day—even when the world tells you to sit down. Rockstar Confidence is the ultimate power source behind change-making women. It's your edge. Your fire. Your revolution. If you're an entrepreneur, trailblazer, founder, visionary, woman who's ready to stop playing small, stand up, show up, and start leading like a legend... then you're not just confident. You're Rockstar confident.

My firm belief is that serving and uplifting others is one of my superpowers. Founding I Am Unbreakable has allowed me to follow my dream of elevating others and creating a space of belonging. I Am Unbreakable is more than just a brand—it's a movement. We ignite the potential of purpose-driven women worldwide. Our mission is to build a legacy of confident, connected women who lead with purpose, spark change, and impact future generations through the power of storytelling and authentic leadership. But even now, I know that I am more, and I know that I can do more. I have drawn my line in the sand, and I know my boundaries. I believe in my business, and I trust myself more than ever. I believe in the profound power of sisterhood. You know your front-row sisters. We form meaningful connections, collaborate every chance we get, and create unbreakable communities just like this one.

Understand that you are also a Rockstar. You are here, and if you're reading this book, you have an innate knowledge that you are ready to take on the world. The truth about you is that you already have the grit, resilience, fearlessness, and love in your heart. You don't have to decide everything about your future right now. How will you go about finding what you're looking for next?

That's the million-dollar question. One thing with you that I know for sure is that most are looking for the exact same thing. Belonging. That was my purpose in creating I Am Unbreakable. It was born from a vision of *Sex and the City* meets *The View*. It's a bold, unfiltered, and authentic relationship-based conversation between besties who help each other rise and thrive. I Am Unbreakable is not just a brand, it's a global movement for women who lead, build, and break the mold.

For those who are:

Ready to lead bolder.

Ready to turn resilience into your superpower.

Ready to join the women rewriting what's possible.

Our Front Row Sisters is a powerhouse community of women who don't just clap for each other—they *build empires together*.

Even when I tape my podcasts, people ask me, "Are you going to edit that out?" And I say, "No, I'm not." I tell them, when you start editing out little things, your audience notices. They can tell you're trying to hide something. So what if the UPS guy rings the doorbell? Or the dog barks? Or your kid cries? Or you need to breastfeed? That's life. Being able to be your true, authentic self is so empowering!

It's funny, every time I speak, the takeaway is very, very similar: show up for yourself, show up how you feel comfortable, and remember not to get caught up in outside influences. I often talk to the audience about why I love wearing white, specifically that I wear white all year long, especially in winter.

It pisses certain people off and empowers others. I find that so interesting. I show up in white (designer, ripped jeans), a leather jacket, a diamond choker, and a Blondie, Rolling Stones, or Rock 'n' Roll tee. I throw in some Louis Vuitton, a little flair and pizzazz, and I show up the way I want to.

People have told me my whole life, "You've got to wear a suit. You can't wear that. You've got to wear a dress." No. I'm going to show up however I please, respectfully, professionally, and authentically.

I can't tell you how many messages I get: *"Wearing white pants today — thank you!"* or *"Where do I get that leather jacket for next week's conference?"* because we've been suppressed by the idea that to be professional means dressing a certain way.

I remember doing a brand photoshoot, and my photographer, who I love, texted, *"Bring a suit. We'll shoot it sexy, nothing underneath, keep it open, we'll do some bling."* I pushed back. I'm so glad I did. After five shoots together, she said to me, "You've just found who you are. Who you are is authentically you. Don't change that."

I once freaked her out with a two-piece outfit—the top looked like a disco ball, tiny silver tiles, mini skirt, the whole nine yards. She loved it. I told her, "I got this just for you."

Society gives us norms. But who even made those norms? As Patrick Swayze's character in the movie *Dirty Dancing* famously said, "Nobody puts Baby in a corner," and nobody should put you in a box either.

I don't fit in a box. If something interesting is happening, I'll circle the perimeter, at best. Otherwise, I'll just be me. I know I'm not for everybody, just like you won't be for everybody. But just knowing that is incredibly powerful. You don't have to be for everyone. As long as you go to bed at night and feel good about how you showed up, and you wake up and still feel the same way, then guess what? You've done your job. You're living like a Rockstar. And you've been true to yourself.

When I talk about being unbreakable, people say to me, "Oh my God, you're so strong. You're so well-spoken." And then they say, "I'm such an introvert. I'm so shy. I could never..."

There it is again—those words. *I am shy.* I told myself the same thing for years. You know my story about Tony Robbins? He said, "The thing you fear most is what you want most."

It's true. I tell people: If you only knew how I felt before my first big keynote—I hadn't slept in three days. I threw up the morning of. I considered vodka and orange juice as a breakfast smoothie (lol). I was terrified. They look at me, shocked. "Are you kidding?" Nope. Even Mick Jagger gets stage fright. Everybody does. I've just reframed it as excitement. It's adrenaline. It's my body preparing to leave it all on the stage for my audience. Every time before I go on stage, I take five to fifteen minutes alone. No makeup artist. No questions. I need to Zen out so I can show up for others wholly and authentically.

At a recent event, I was there as the media partner for a good friend and mentor, Deborah. Hundreds of people were there. She said, "I just want to sit here for a second."

I said, "Then sit."

I got her something to eat. She sat for about forty minutes, did a quick touch-up, and then stepped out on stage like a Rockstar, glowing with energy, in her beautiful bright pink suit. She was unstoppable.

Later, she thanked me, saying, "Thank you for guiding me to take that time for myself." That messaging was so important for me to hear. It was another sign that I was guiding others in the correct way. Back to themselves, to align with their energy. When she showed up, she over-delivered because she took the time she needed to serve others. Now that is definitely a Rockstar.

Giving yourself grace and space to pause, to breathe, to center, is one of the most empowering things you can do.

My next tattoo? *"Life's a journey, not a destination."* Some people do the same thing for thirty, forty, or seventy years. Maybe they're happy. Maybe they regret it. But if you have a dream, follow it. Never give up on yourself. Anything you believe is possible *is* possible—with grit, with your girl gang, with your family, with alignment. But you have to live like you already *are* that person.

I'll share a funny story. I mentioned earlier that I got my magazine in Chapters and Indigo. Even before I had a distribution deal, I'd take a copy into the store, wait until no one was looking, and slide it onto the shelf. I knew it would be there one day. Didn't know how. But I believed.

One of the last times I did this, I heard cheering. I thought, *Maybe it's for me?* Of course it wasn't. But I went downstairs and guess who was there? Heather, the CEO of Indigo. Just roaming the store. I believed it was a sign. And you know what? I was right.

You didn't become a Rockstar the moment someone noticed you. You were always the Rockstar. You just had to remember who you are. I've walked through chaos. I've sat in the silence after everything fell apart. I've rebuilt from the ruins more times than I can count. And through it all, one truth kept rising: *You don't need permission to rise.* You already are the comeback.

This book wasn't written from a pedestal—it was written from the trenches. From the raw, unfiltered, battle-tested truth of what it takes to believe in yourself when nobody else does. When the lights are off. When your name's not called. When the dream feels heavy and the doubt feels louder than the fire in your gut. But you didn't quit. You didn't crumble. You kept showing up. Even bruised. Even breathless.

And *that* is Rockstar Confidence. It's not a mood—it's a mission. It's the decision to stand tall in a world that benefits when you play small. It's the energy that says: *I know who I am. I know why I'm here. And I will not be silenced.*

Listen. Confidence isn't handed to you. It's built. Built in heartbreak. Built in rejection. Built in every moment you whispered, "I've got me," when no one else did. I'm not here to hand you motivation. I'm here to remind you of what you already know deep down: You're a damn force. You've already survived what was meant to destroy you. You've already risen after what tried to bury you. You've already shown the world that your power can't be stolen, bought, or faked. This is your edge. Your superpower.

ROCKSTAR RECAP

You don't need permission to rise. You already are the comeback.

Being unbreakable is about resilience and knowing that no matter what life throws at you, you're going to be okay. It's about rising again and again, with clarity, compassion, and conviction.

Journal Prompts For Readers

★ What does unbreakable mean to you today?
___
___
___

★ What boundaries make you stronger?
___
___
___

★ Where are you ready to go?
___
___
___

★ Where are you ready to rise again?
___
___
___

Make Your Move
Write your personal unbreakable manifesto, a one-paragraph declaration of who you are, what you stand for, and what comes next and why you know you are a Rockstar.

CONCLUSION
YOU WERE ALWAYS THE ROCKSTAR

"Vulnerability is the birthplace of innovation, creativity, and change."
~ Brené Brown

The real magic starts the moment you decide to believe in yourself. When you take the risk, bet on yourself, and stop waiting for someone else to name your worth, *you rise*. Loving yourself isn't soft. It's the boldest move you'll ever make. Because showing up for yourself, every single day, is how you build the kind of confidence that can't be shaken. And when you live like a Rockstar, you stop surviving—and start owning every damn stage you step on.

This entire journey, every messy chapter, every late night, every tear behind closed doors, was never about becoming someone else. It was about becoming *you*. The real You. The unfiltered, unshakable, bold-as-hell version of you that was never meant to play it safe, shrink, or stay silent. The world told you to dim it down. To wait your turn. To earn your worth. To be less. And you? You burned that script. Because here's the truth: confidence isn't found in applause. It's built in silence. In chaos. In grit. In courage. In those moments where everything felt like it was falling apart, and you showed up anyway. No spotlight. No validation. Just you and the fire in your chest saying, *Today I rise.*

You don't need someone else to hand you a stage. You are the stage. You don't need a title to lead. You are the leader. You followed the dream that kept whispering, "There's more." And guess what? There is. There always was. You dared to believe that your story, even the broken parts, had purpose. And that belief? That's your power.

Resilience isn't something you build once. It's a decision you make over and over again. You were always the Rockstar. Even when you were still learning the chords. Even when your voice cracked. Even when the lights were off and no one was watching. So now, walk into that room like it's already yours. Take the mic. Take up space. Take the damn lead. You don't owe the world perfection. You owe yourself your truth. And your truth is this: *You are unbreakable. You are legendary. You are the fire. You are the comeback. You are the confidence. You are the movement. You were always the Rockstar.*

Now? *You rise.* To keep going. To rise through the setbacks. To show up for yourself with a heart wide open and a spine made of steel.

They'll say you're lucky. But you know better. *Luck didn't build this—you did.* Through sacrifice, mistakes, grace, guts, and ten thousand comebacks. You didn't just get through the storm—you became the storm. Let them underestimate you. That's always been your advantage. Let them call you "too much." That just means you're full of something they've never had the courage to claim. Let this be your reminder: you were never meant to blend in. You were built to stand out. To stand up. To stand tall.

I tell people they're a Rockstar all the time, when they've done something fantastic, when they're suffering, or when they just look like they need a little reminder that they are strong. It's kind of like walking into Disney World. *Magic happens.* They light up. They feel it. Even if they respond with a "No, I'm not," the truth still lands. That tiny spark still hits. That's the power of positive affirmation. You are unbreakable. And the confidence that comes from practicing these affirmations daily? It shows up in spades.

Remember: *confidence is a promise you make to yourself and keep, when no one else is watching.*

Working through obstacles and realizing that resilience is a decision, that you grow through adversity, is one of the most powerful gifts you can give yourself. The more you face the tough stuff, the more you know that even when life hits hard, you'll be okay. You can do hard things. You can follow your dreams. If you've got a passion burning inside, whether it's to own a small bookstore, speak on global stages, be a stay-at-home parent, or coach your kid's hockey team, if it keeps tugging at your heart no matter how often you try to bury it, that's your clue. That's the direction to explore.

Be curious. Be your own private investigator. Gather the evidence. Trace the clues that life is placing in front of you, just like I've done. Every time I ignored my gut, my woman's intuition whispered louder. And the moment I started listening? Everything shifted. Your most peaceful, most transformative moments will come when you stop asking the world for permission and start trusting the voice inside yourself.

Maybe that's why *The Wizard of Oz* meant so much to me. So many powerful messages: there's no place like home, the value of trusted friendships, and most importantly, that the power was always within you. You've always had what it takes to create the life you dream of. Now you've got the tools to prove it.

So remember my three favorite words: *Yes, You Can.*

I want to thank you. I'm incredibly grateful that you've spent this time with me, reading my story and listening to the stories of others. I hope this journey gives you space to reflect, to feel seen, and to feel empowered. I hope it gave you what you needed in the moment you needed it. There is so much power in showing up for yourself first. But if there are days you can't even put your feet on the floor, and life still demands something from you—an event, a workday, a kid to take somewhere, a dog to walk—show up for someone else. There is deep, rewarding beauty in being of service, especially when it's hard.

There have been days when I didn't want to show up. And I did it anyway. That's the difference. That's what the one-percenters do. And maybe where you are today is right in that tough space. You had a fight with your partner. You didn't sleep. You don't feel your best. There are a million reasons not to show up. Do it anyway. Then go home. Reflect. Notice what came from showing up. You made a difference. And you trained your brain to believe that *Yes, You Can*.

We've all been through hard times. The world is uncertain. But when you keep showing up, especially when it's hard, you build something indestructible inside of you. You build self-belief. Even if you're not seeing all the results yet, show up anyway. Your efforts compound. They come back multiplied. One day, you'll look around and realize: *I'm living it.*

I hope you'll reach out to me and share your story. Because your story matters. People need to hear it. Humanity thrives on realness. On truth. On hope. And on reminders that we've all struggled and we've all gotten back up.

Just like I hope my story has touched lives, *your story will too*. So, from one resilient soul to another, I see you. I believe in you.

Rockstar Rising isn't just a book—it's a movement. It's about owning your story, believing in yourself hard, and choosing courage over comfort every damn time. This is where confidence is built—not in the spotlight, but in the moments no one sees. *I am* isn't just a statement. It's your power source. When you love yourself, bet on yourself, and walk like it already belongs to you, everything changes. You're not just rising. You're leading like a legend.

If this book cracked something open inside you, *good*. That fire you feel? That's not hype. That's your power waking up. I wrote this for the women who've been underestimated, overlooked, and told to wait their turn. The ones who kept going when no one was watching. The women who carried trauma, rejection, and doubt, and still showed up. Confidence isn't born—it's built in chaos. And if you've been through it? You already have what it takes.

Your struggle wasn't the setback—it was the setup for your rise.

You didn't pick up this book for fluff or inspiration. You picked it up because you're done waiting. Done playing by rules you never agreed to. Done shrinking. Done hiding. Done making yourself small to keep others comfortable.

You're ready to build something legendary from everything they thought would break you. This isn't self-help. This is self-leadership. Confidence without conditions. Power without permission. Clarity without apology.

You don't need a map—you are the blueprint. You don't need more credentials—you need to trust your own fire. And if the world hasn't made space for your voice yet? Good. You're here to build your own damn stage.

This book will challenge you, shake you, and call you up—if you let it. Here's the truth: You're not here to be chosen. You're here to choose yourself. You're not here to chase confidence. You're here to own it. You're not here to blend in. You're here to lead out loud. You're not waiting to become a Rockstar. You already are.

Let's rise.

BONUS CHAPTERS

CHAPTER THIRTEEN
YOUR PERSONAL PRIVATE INVESTIGATOR

We used to live simple lives. People married each other for fifty years, went to work, came home, and hung out with friends and neighbors. There was no Internet or Facebook or TikTok, which opened ordinary lives to the entire world ... of possibilities.

A fast-paced world of endless choices means we live in a far different way now. Everything moves at a supersonic speed, meaning more roadblocks or difficult life moments and decisions.

Don't feel bad if your life seems to be one crisis after another.

All of us find ourselves at certain crisis moments in life where it seems like things will never be okay or "normal" again. Maybe you're asking yourself: *Is my husband cheating? Is my kid on drugs? How will I get through this divorce and keep custody of my kids? Is someone stealing from me? Is that woman I met online and seems so perfect the real thing? Did he really steal money from me? Where does my mate go when he or she disappears for an hour each night?*

Maybe it's time to hire a P.I. or read a book about one. That brings me to this time.

For so many years, I've been asked to write a book about my experiences leading the agency while also providing concrete tips on how to deal with some of life's biggest challenges. I call them "red flag" moments where everything can pivot on a dime, including new relationships, divorce, business hurdles, child safety, and dealing with questionable behavior even if you've known the other person for decades.

I sat down to write a book with the goal of giving you a deep look into these universal topics. I wanted to share client stories and then explain if there is anything to be done to prevent these situations. Most of all, I wanted to explore on these pages how you can handle these situations if confronted with what might be unimaginable. Quite often, your quick response to life's red flags and crisis moments is instrumental when it comes to the end result.

Along the way, I'll give you some insights into my own life as a busy, working mother, along with my special **P.I. Tips,** pull-out suggestions that you can go back to—again and again—for quick refreshers. Those pull-out tips are crucial for those three in the morning moments when you have to act as your own P.I.

Quick note: My advice does not replace hiring your own private investigator, but it will give you an insider view into how P.I.s work, think, and deal with stumbling blocks big and small. My hope is that the pages you will read will serve as a foundation where you can avoid trouble or see it coming from a mile away. In other words, stop the bleeding (emotionally and financially) before it's a gusher. Instead of allowing a situation to morph and change with time, I hope the stories, suggestions, and, yes, "tricks of the P.I. trade" that you read here will help you swerve from trouble, avoid risky choices, and live in a way where you feel better about your choices.

Is it possible to live risk-free in this unpredictable world? Probably not.

The win is having the knowledge and peace of mind to deal with anything and everything thrown at you in the smartest way, where you step into the power position. Knowledge is power. It's also freedom from fear.

CHAPTER FOURTEEN
RED FLAG MOMENTS

A recent reboot episode of *Sex and the City* had the character of Miranda Hobbs standing in front of her lover, who is irate. For three weeks, they've been having sex, but only one of them has been upfront. "You're in an open marriage, right?" Che asks Miranda, who looks as if the weight of her current guilt will crush her soul. "Let me make one thing clear. I'm a lot of things. But I'm not a liar, and I'm not a cheater! I don't break up marriages!" Che insists.

If only this was the prevailing attitude about infidelity. It's not, which is why cheating outside of one's marriage is the top reason my phone rings all day long. Men and women alike call me because they need to know. Are they? Or aren't they? Can this marriage be saved?

The stats are not encouraging to those who believe in fidelity. In fact, infidelity in Canada is so prevalent that one in ten Canadians have admitted to cheating on their partner, and over 20 percent claim to have seriously considered doing so. The study focused on physical cheating, but we will soon learn that there are different types of straying.

It really bucks the saying, Ain't love grand?

Love can be lovely, or it can leave one of the partners feeling like they were blindsided by a truck. Others at the other end of the line can barely sob out the words, "I think my husband is cheating on me, but I'm not sure how to prove it."

Finally, there is that client facing an infidelity situation with rage in their hearts. I'll hear, "I need you to get that bastard." Or maybe it's, "I've been dying to leave that bitch, and now she gave me a reason. I caught her in bed with the neighbor, and now I'm out!"

The stories are all epic tales. There was the realtor who found her husband in bed with another man, who informed the crushed wife, "We want everything. We want the condo, plus the bedroom drapes. You have very good taste."

At one time, she did.

In men.

WHO CHEATS MORE—MEN OR WOMEN?

This is a tough question. The straight answer is: It's complicated. Studies over the years have attempted to understand more about the cheating gender divide, and an overwhelming number of them suggest that men are more prone to cheating than woman. However, there are factors to consider because infidelity isn't just cut and dry.

It begins by understanding what you consider cheating. Of course, it's cheating if your wife is sharing bed space at a local inn on the weekends with a secret lover. But what if he stays up all night on Facebook typing private, emotional, and/or flirty words to a former girlfriend or someone new? Is it flirting or more when she has a "work husband" to share all her private thoughts, complaints, and daily hurdles? Is it infidelity if he is just as "married" to a slew of women he never met but visits nightly on porn sites?

Women typically view an emotional affair as more serious, while men are more concerned by physical cheating, such as sex with another partner. One interesting fact is that gender can play a part in the admission of cheating behavior, with men more likely than females to admit that they've done the marriage wrong.

Another sad fact is that women are hardly ever the only blameless victims. Studies show that women are cheating at a rate 40 percent higher than they did 40 years ago. I do have to keep an open mind about those numbers since now women have far more discussions where they're open and frank about sexuality. No longer is an affair just for them to remember. Several girlfriends and others often know about it before the husband is enlightened.

A client of mine liked to have outdoor sex. Imagine her despair when she was having sex with a dad from school on the hood of her car in a public park. She had no idea that her father-in-law walked the dog so late at night. But she figured that out when the 80-year-old tapped her sweaty shoulder and said, "Lynn, is that you?"

CHEATING PARTNERS ARE EVERYWHERE

Many people believe infidelity revolves around clandestine meetings in faraway hotels where it's a quick sex session and then goodbye. The cheating game has changed for both men and women, who often treat cheating in the same way that they treat dating. Let's look at the ways:

Dating sites and apps. These were designed to make it easier for single people to find a partner, yet they've been infiltrated by many marrieds who are looking for ways to combat the boredom and "is that all there is" vibe in their lives. Some are looking for a relationship that will remain private and serve as a diversion to their marriages. Others crave a quick hookup or even a texting or online relationship to fill in the gaps. Perhaps their marriage is loveless now. The whirlwind romance of an online love suddenly can make life exciting again. Many cheaters find that the idea of hiding this affair just ups the ante and makes it even more thrilling.

The one that got away. The truth is that marriage can become a daily routine of kids, food, house, and work, followed by kids, kids, and more kids. It's exhausting and stressful and often begins to feel like each day is an exact duplicate of the last one. Then, one night you notice that Bob from high school is on Facebook. It's not harmful to reach out to your high school boyfriend to see what he's doing today, one might reason. A few weeks later and you're pouring out your hopes and dreams while deleting the evidence. The point is many people cheat with those who should probably remain in the past. It's not good for a marriage when an ex is suddenly in the mix, and it's often just a matter of time until talking turns into sex and then divorce.

Opportunities run amok. Perhaps you're on the school board, and there is that one mom who flirts like crazy with you. It makes your wife nuts, and you ignore it in her presence, but now suddenly you're seeing her at that holiday party. She's in a little red dress, and you can't get her out of your mind. The point is potential cheating partners are everywhere. You can't micro-manage every single person who comes into your spouse's orbit, but you can keep your eyes open. Later on, when the cheating is revealed, many wives or husbands say to me, "I had a bad feeling all along that this other person would try to break up our marriage."

SO, WHAT KIND OF AFFAIR IS IT?

It helps to start by defining what kind of infidelity is lurking in a relationship. Here are a few possibilities.

Emotional Affairs

There are all kinds of ways people cheat these days. In fact, many women and men ask me if their partner is "really cheating" after they find long dialogs on Facebook Messenger with strangers. A client asked me, "Why is my wife suddenly pouring out her heart to this man I don't know? She grumbles a few words to me when we pass each other in the hallways. And then I find her at midnight talking to Bill about her day, her friends, her hopes, and her dreams of the future." The plethora of social media makes it very easy to have what's called an emotional affair. You don't see the person; they don't see you. There is the protection of both of you out there in cyberland, which makes it far easier to share feelings. There are also very few consequences. When this emotional affair bores you … Just go on to the next. It's not a divorce. It's a deletion. Emotional affairs are just as hurtful as physical ones. Your mate might or might not be doing the naked dance with this person, but they are sharing an intimacy that might be lacking in the marriage.

Here are my thoughts about Facebook: Absolutely, you should be concerned if your spouse is spending a lot of time on Facebook, especially if they're reconnecting with someone from the past. A lot of affairs of the heart begin as emotional affairs online through the simple push of a button. You've reconnected with your high school boy- or girlfriend. Now what? It's typical to start off as old flames just checking out each other's adult lives. Maybe you went to a reunion with the person and agreed to stay in better touch. It seems unassuming and innocent … but is it really innocent to tell someone else you once had interest in about your marriage, your dreams, your heart, your soul? That sounds a lot like dating.

My professional opinion is that someone who is not getting attention at home will reach out online to find others who will pay them attention. They will look in the cyber world for what they are missing. Again, what starts out innocently might not end that way.

I wouldn't want my husband to talk to old girlfriends online, and he wouldn't do it because it would cause a rift between us.

Physical Affairs

Abby and David lived in a lovely townhouse community with their young son, Mark. For years, their next-door neighbor Ginger behaved in a vaguely inappropriate way. Some of her greatest "hits" included walking around in a flimsy robe with nothing underneath or asking David to come over to her house. Divorced for years, she would need constant help, which often turned into a glass of wine or an hour-long session about work, life, and love. It took about a year before David was sneaking next door to add sex to the mix. Another incredible case had a client's high school girlfriend moving next door to a couple in order to "get him back." She also played the helpless act until they were having a physical affair. Another client knew his wife was sneaking down the street to have sex with an unmarried doctor. The point is physical affairs are always in the realm of possibility. If you think something could be happening, there is a good chance that it's not just your imagination.

Exes

Many happily married partners fall into the trap of having sex again with an ex. Maybe the exes are stuck having meetings about their children, and they have a lapse of reason. Or perhaps it's a case of one of the exes not being happy with their current situation and longing for the old way of life. There are many exes who make it extremely hard on the new wife, including Gina, who used to do the child hand-off each Sunday while either wearing a string bikini or just a towel. Brazen about the effect she thought she was having on her ex-husband, she allowed her new husband to watch while announcing to both, "I'm the hottest piece either of you will ever have." Talk about family bonding! Exes who keep it out there that they're available need to be told definitely that it's over. Even a quick insult might make them stop. Imagine the situation in the string bikini with the ex-husband remarking, "Did you gain a few pounds?"

NINE SIGNS OF A CHEATING SPOUSE

We've seen the cheating scenario play out in our favorite movies. Boy meets girl. Girl marries boy. Boy starts sleeping with that hot woman at work. This might seem like Hollywood fodder, but it's the hard truth for many who have seen their "rock star" relationships collapse in a sea of hurt and betrayal.

Of course, every situation is different, and while no signs are definitive, private investigators know that there are certain telltale behaviors that can indicate a cheating partner. Here are nine signs of a cheating spouse so that you can be one step ahead of being blindsided by a cheater.

1. **Password-protected electronics.** You know he or she is cheating when they have made their electronics off-limits to you. You can't access their phone, tablet, or computer because suddenly these things fall into the password-protected zone. Or perhaps the password that they've used for years and shared with you has been purposely changed. You ask for the new one in order to check the hockey scores and are greeted with a quick, "I'll check the scores later. This is a cheater's favorite way to keep a big part of their life private. Another sign of a cheater is someone who carries their phone into the bathroom and spends quite a lot of time in there texting a lover or girlfriend or boyfriend. Someone who insists on catching up on email late at night in private has their reasons why they need to be alone.
2. **Sudden attention to their appearance.** Perhaps your significant other has let things "go" over the years when it comes to their body. Ten extra pounds has led to twenty or thirty. All of a sudden, he or she has taken on a renewed and maybe even obsessive interest in going to the gym and buying new and perhaps sexy clothes. They hired a trainer or are spending too much time at the gym, which is a meat market of cheating. They're on the lettuce diet. Their hair is different now, and so are their only grooming habits. He takes two showers a day now and wears this funky cologne.

A sudden change in appearance can signal that he or she is trying to look good ... for someone else.

3. **Changes in your sex life.** It's natural for the frequency of sex in a marriage to ebb and flow over time, but a significant dip or spike in intimacy can indicate that someone is having an affair. The increased and unexplained effort in the bedroom can be the direct result of a guilty spouse. Or perhaps new bedroom behaviors and/or routines have been introduced by an outside source to create a different way of having sex. Perhaps this wasn't present in your sex life before, such as new positions, sex toys, different or public locations, talk of adding a third party into the mix, aggressive sex, sharing dirty talk, and interest in having an open marriage filled with new partners. The flipside is a sex life that has all but dried up because one of the two partners is getting their needs met elsewhere.

4. **A sudden change of habits.** You've been doing the "I think we're happily ever after for years under one roof," which means you know her daily habits. She always makes coffee at home; he never exercises before bed. He rarely gets phone calls at night; she never sits on the couch and texts her mother. It's normal to change your habits from time to time over the course of your life, but an abrupt change of behavior could be a sign of infidelity. Maybe your partner has joined a gym, but you don't see any progress over several months even though they're gone two hours a night, three nights a week. A series of habit changes over a short period of time might be a cause for concern. Beverly thought it was odd that her husband suddenly needed to walk the dog at 10 at night instead of 8, when they always went together. It didn't take much to figure out that he was calling a woman at 10 while Fido did his business.

5. **Changes in attitude.** Just like habits, attitudes can change for any number of reasons. Maybe he is under a lot of pressure at work, or she didn't get that coveted job. Only the marrieds in a couple know what's a truly unusual attitude versus just a small roadblock. Cheating partners will sometimes experience unexplained mood swings, ranging from hostile and frustrated to overly affectionate and bubbly. You can blame the combination of adrenaline and guilt associated with having an affair. Or, perhaps your partner is suddenly insecure or has a sudden dip in self-esteem due to the cheating.
6. **Lying, avoidance, and insincerity.** Many cheaters want it both ways. They like being married but want some thrills on the side. In order to live both lives, they become James Bonds in their efforts to cover their tracks. This might include telling lies, deflecting, and acting defensive when questioned about their time and behavior. Just a simple question will make them explode. "How was that late meeting?" you ask. He snaps and yells, "Fine! How do you think it was? Do you think I want to be there?" If this is out of character, the reason might be that he or she is dealing with spiraling guilt, stress, and the tangled web of keeping all of his or her lies straight. Most likely, a cheater won't answer questions with more than a quick word or two. "How was your run? You were out there forever," you comment. She snaps, "Yes." Once, you had a sincere and intimate relationship with your partner, which has been reduced to one-word statements.
7. **Periods where your spouse is unreachable or unavailable.** In the past, you called him twice a day at work and chatted for a few minutes about future plans. Or it was your pattern to always talk on her drive home. Suddenly, your partner is unavailable, and the excuses fly. He was talking to his mother; she forgot to charge her phone. Both were busy,

busy, busy. Your spouse should be available to you. Red flags need to fly when he or she won't talk or can barely talk or your talk time has been replaced by something or someone new.

8. **Unexplained credit card charges or hidden statement.** Here's the kind of proof that they find in movies about cheating. The wife or husband pulls out a credit card statement, and there are charges that include lingerie or hotel rooms or fancy dinners that didn't include the other spouse. A tell-tale sign of cheating is when the credit card bills used to arrive by mail but now are suddenly sent to her email or work address. Sure, some of us have gone paperless to save the environment. Cheaters go paperless to save themselves from the trail of lies followed by the tears. Also, watch for a spouse who takes out a lot of cash via the ATM to make sure they always have money for meals and rooms. It might be worth questioning why your spouse needs all of that cash to get through the week.

9. **Check your tech.** All of us are connected now and living our lives on social media. Spouses who are cheating make sure to conceal incidences of infidelity by changing their passwords on a regular basis, clearing their browser history, and making sure that their social media accounts are private. A big red flag is a spouse who has removed the other spouse from photos and unchecked the "married" box on their profiles.

TRUSTING YOUR GUT

I've spoken to thousands of spouses who look and sound like they were punched in the gut. "I never saw the signs," I'll hear. Of course, a large part of clients remain in denial because their feelings have been minimized. One client told me, "My husband called me crazy jealous for thinking he was cheating, but deep down, I always had this feeling that he was cheating on me. He made me think I was nuts." It's sad because I always tell people that if they have a gut feeling—a Spidey sense or intuition—that you must honor those feelings and explore them. If your body, mind, heart, and soul tell you that something is wrong, it is wrong. Or can be wrong.

Of course, there are times when infidelity is NOT what's happening. The other day, a middle-aged man called me and said, "I'm one thousand percent convinced that my wife is cheating on me. She lost a lot of weight. She's dressing fancy. Wearing perfume. I can't find the credit card bill. In fact, I discovered that she re-routed the bill, so the credit card statement came to her work."

"Her electronics?" I asked.

"Password protected, and only she knows the password," he said.

It sounded exactly like infidelity, but I still needed to keep an open mind. Always innocent until proven guilty is my motto.

My investigators and I came to find out that his wife didn't have an outside lover or even an emotional crutch. She had a shopping addiction. The good news is that he was relieved and they stayed together. The bad news was he was suddenly $240,000 in debt.

It's always something, but it's not always what you think it is—and that's the truth.

TWO CASE STUDIES:

Two's Company; Three's a Crowd

People often believe that infidelity is between a husband and wife and/or boyfriend and girlfriend. However, a lot of times I get a call from the mistress who is now worried that the husband she's bedding is now cheating on her with another mistress. In one case, Gwen (the mistress) contacted us because she suspected that her boyfriend, who was married, had that other "other" person on the side. She decided to play P.I. and followed him around for two days and watched him walking through a park with a beautiful red-haired woman who was not the wife. Plus, he saw Gwen every single day for lunch at some motel or hotel, but now it was down to twice a week because he had work meetings.

It was true that he was seeing a second mistress. Photos confirmed that she was his Tuesday-Thursday hotel gal, while Gwen was Monday-Wednesday, and the wife got the rest of his attention on Fridays-Monday. Sunday was apparently a well-earned day of rest! In the end, Gwen sent the new photos to the man's wife, who was fine with this arrangement as long as he was tested for AIDS once a week. Yet, he was upset with Gwen and cut her loose, citing "trust issues."

Moral of the story: You can't trust the person you're cheating with because they might just be in a hotel parking lot grabbing the ass of another.

The Mail Order Bride

A lovely woman retained our services because she needed to know if her husband was cheating. From all appearances, she was the perfect wife and mother of four beautiful kids. She lived an amazing life with her family, including their eight-million-dollar mansion on the lake, travel, and friends. Yet, she felt something hollow each day when he would kiss her and go downtown to his condo office, where he often worked until the middle of the night.

She even asked her husband if he was cheating, and he confessed. "I made a mistake," he said with tears rolling down his face. "Please don't leave me." The truth was she was what they call a mail-order bride from another country. She didn't plan to leave him but admitted to me that she would never trust him again.

I thought the case was settled until a week later when she called me back.

"I have this feeling," she began, "I don't know if I'm crazy."

"Let's check it out," I said because now I was getting a bad feeling.

Sure enough, we found out very quickly that the husband was still with the same mistress, who basically lived in the condo office. She had every intention of breaking up his marriage and moving into the big house, but our mail-order bride thought differently. She decided to stay in name only, whether they had a real marriage or not. He didn't care. He now had permission to lead a double life as long as he never touched his wife again.

Next chapter: More infidelity stories and how to deal with a cheating heart.

CHAPTER FIFTEEN
HOT P.I. TOPICS

Once upon a time, there was a wealthy businessman who adored his teacher wife. Unfortunately, she was having a fling with the principal at the Catholic school where she worked. The husband was a European man who was willing to forgive her for her "sins," although it wasn't easy. He told me the sad truth, which was that his own children went to school in the area, and many knew about this affair. It wouldn't be easy for the family to save face, but he still loved his wife. "Listen," he told her, "I haven't been 100 percent perfect either when it comes to being faithful. I'm willing to forgive you if you're willing to forgive me."

They mutually agreed to own their past mistakes, blaming it on their European tempers and passions along with a healthy dose of extremely bad judgement. I suggested counseling as a way to talk through their problems, and they decided it was a good idea for both the parents and those kids, three of them, ages four to thirteen.

He was my client, and I suggested that he track his life.

"I'm going to trust her blindly," he said. "We need to trust each other."

A few therapy sessions later, and he called me again. "Something still doesn't feel right," he said.

This time, my company did the tracking and we caught her after school having sex with the principal in the parking lot of a local mall. We filmed them and sadly gave the client the bad news. Shockingly, he was going to forgive her again, but she took a pass on the plan.

"It is what it is," she said. "There is nothing you can really do."

Our client was such a nice man, and a good-looking one, who had been burned twice, which is not unusual. "I'll never love again," he vowed to us. And this was before the wife suddenly remembered that he had abused her. A lot of times, police charges are made when a couple is splitting. Allegations tend to fly, and our client vehemently denied ever abusing his wife. Her charges stemmed from a day at the local print shop when he grabbed papers out of her hand; thus, the abuse.

The first thing I tell my clients is to buy a hidden pocket voice-activated recorder for "run-ins" with their soon-to-be ex. Many spouses know that you cannot get your breakup partner out of the house by simply saying he or she screwed around on you. The only way to get them out in places like Canada and beyond is to charge them with violence or threatening the other party in a way that makes them feel unsafe.

By the way, my client did buy the recorder, and it became clear to the police that he did not abuse his wife.

Yes, he was coached, educated, and informed.

Think of the following pages as Infidelity—the Advanced Course. It's about making the smartest moves possible to have the best results for you and your family.

P.I. Tip: *It's always something ... but not necessarily what you think it is. If it is cheating on your marital vows, then you can do two things: turn a blind eye and ignore it or call it a day with the relationship. In my opinion, cheating is a betrayal. If you cannot recover or heal or deal with the betrayal, then you should end it.*

BE YOUR OWN P.I.—HELL, NO!

We've all seen that movie scene where someone might be cheating and the other party goes on this mission to find out. All of a sudden, they go into untrained private detective mode, and they're sneaking all over the city, trying to take photographs, digging through credit card receipts, and generally playing detective with no formal training. This is a great way to drive yourself crazy, get caught, and never get the evidence and/or break your own heart.

I've seen regular people try to go into detective mode, and it always ends up in an ugly mess. It's not like you would even consider becoming your own brain surgeon, which is far more serious, but you get the idea.

Infidelity investigations are like opening Pandora's box. You want to go to a professional who will be discreet. Do it yourself and you'll end up flagging the other parties and putting them on high alert, which might just prove to be an expensive or emotionally hurtful mistake. Or embarrassing. Take the wife who thought she was calling her husband's mistress to "give her a piece of my mind" about their affair when she really called his boss. The enraged wife said several unsavory things to the boss before being told of her mistake. In the end, the husband was assigned to a different work team, with his boss citing a general awkwardness now. Eventually, he left the company, which meant less income for the now-divorcing family.

Word to the wise: A pro wouldn't make this mistake or a confrontational call.

What should you do if you have suspicions? Take a deep breath and put a lid on your inner crazy person. Keep a lid on what you found and unload to a professional P.I. in the end; no one will think you're crazy nuts, plus the pros will take your claim and the end result will be the video or photos confirming or not confirming because something else is happening, or maybe nothing is going on.

A lot of people are afraid of the truth and sit on the information. All in good time. What comes next is up to you. In some cases, it's best to wait and not put the cart before the horse. If something still doesn't sit well after a period of time, then it's time to call the professionals.

There are also people who reach out to a P.I. with no direct evidence of an affair. They didn't find that weird hotel receipt or a stray hairband in the car. Yet, something is not sitting right about life in general. This is the right time to go to a specialist rather than live in this limbo. So many times, I'll have a client say, "I just have a gut feeling."

I'm so incredibly spiritual that I always say, "Stay in tune with your body. You can tell when things aren't right." This is especially important if a child or children are involved. A lion protects the cubs even if they're "going on a hunch." Do not ignore that little voice. The more you listen, the more you are told.

Your good common sense will also tell you when you need to reach out to a P.I. A client once told me that his wife admitted easily that she has never been faithful to any partner in the past—boyfriend or husband. "She told me she cheated on every single one, but I love her and married her," he lamented. "She told me I was different."

A year into their union, he started to get that sinking feeling, supported by evidence such as his wife suddenly going out once or twice a week with girlfriends. He was a smart guy who came to us and explained the signals he couldn't ignore. And yes, she was cheating on him. Sometimes, a client just needs an outside source like their P.I. to second what they already know is true.

ADVANCED CHEATING 101

In the last chapter, I outlined a few of the most common ways that you can tell if your partner is cheating. The truth is every couple is different—as is their trajectory toward the end of a union. Some people are also better at cheating than others—as if it were a life skill.

Here are a few more advanced ways you can tell if someone is straying:

- **The phone.** Our modern times might exclude holding your partner's hand. But you do hold onto one thing all day long: your phone. I already told you that your partner suddenly changing passwords and not telling you the new one is a reason for suspicion. The same goes with the phone. Those four little numbers to get into a spouse's phone should not be private. It's also unexplainable if your spouse refuses to give you their phone if you need it in a pinch. Let's say you forgot your phone and need to make a quick call. If they go through a song and dance resulting in you not touching their phone, then you might wonder why. I would give my husband the phone in a nanosecond because I have nothing to hide. Let's say he hit the wrong button and checked my texts … No, big deal. I'm not keeping secrets. Also, if your partner takes their cell phone with them everywhere, including the bathroom, I'd wonder. You can put the phone down for a moment because you have no odd instant messages on Facebook, right?
- **Going MIA.** It's not common for responsible adults who are married or in a major relationship to go missing for long or short periods of time unless they star on the show Outlander. You should be able to get in touch with your significant other at all times unless they pilot a 737 or operate on trauma victims. Unless you're married to a president or prime

minister, your partner has the time and permission to pick up a phone that is constantly in their pocket. Most people have a minute or two to answer that phone and say, "I'm good. How are you?" If your partner goes missing on a regular basis, take note and start keeping a journal. Write down the excuses as to why they couldn't answer the phone. Did they really have a flat tire? Again. How could their car battery have no juice for the third time this month? "Sorry babe, I was driving through a bad cell area" only works so many times. Does she have two cell phones?

All I know is my business increased over 600 percent through the pandemic with simple infidelity cases.

P.I. Tip: *Do you see the same strange number popping up on your mate's cell phone again and again? Does this happen at odd hours like midnight or first thing in the morning? Take notice and write the number to give to your P.I. Do not engage in a series of hang-up calls although people do it all the time to no avail.*

- **An emotional mess.** The toll of keeping a secret does an emotional number on the cheater to the point where their basic personality has left the building. Perhaps they're being extra moody to you or even hostile in the home about any little thing. (If the hostility becomes dangerous, then you should call local law enforcement). Does she burst into crying jags for no real reason? Does he blow his top if tonight is chicken and not fish? Is this new to the relationship? If the marital union has mood problems then it might be the guilt of cheating that is making the other partner act in a different way. I'll often remind clients that "moody" shows up in various ways. For example, if your partner is usually a pretty solid, problem-free individual and suddenly they're making issues out of everything, then take note. Yes, every relationship has problems and goes through different phases. A partner magnifying common, everyday issues like the car needing gas or a child's bad grade on one test is overreacting, which isn't the norm. It doesn't mean they're cheating, but there might be something else going on emotionally that's worth digging into to help that person—especially if they're yelling at the kids (see story below).

- **Grandizing someone you know.** Sometimes cheaters are so overwrought with guilt that they will give tiny clues that they're actually cheating. Take the case of Bess, who suddenly couldn't stop talking about their neighbor Ted to her husband. There was Bess telling her husband what a great guy Ted was and how he was so smart and such a great father. It's great to have friends and say nice things about them. It's just that Bess' husband got a little sick of "The Ted Show" at the dinner table or when they were driving and realized Beth went from friends with Ted and his wife to something else. Is your spouse a one-person cheer squad for someone at work? At school? Do they contact each other a lot? See each other? Do they do things without their partners? Those innocent Starbucks chance meetings might not just be the result of fate and needing a little caffeine kick in the morning.

P.I. Tip: *Most of us have perfected the art of having attention to detail at work. Ask yourself from time to time: Do you pay attention to the details of what's going on under your own roof, or have you become complacent over the years?*

CASE STUDY: THE MAJOR OVERREACTOR

A woman called me because her husband was "acting funny," but there was nothing comedic about it. "I think he is a sex addict," she says, "along with having issues with coke and alcohol." This was one of those three in the morning calls that I answered. I settled in, knowing it was going to be a long night.

I could feel her relief as the story poured out over the phone lines.

It wasn't so much all his weekends away for work or his credit cards with the flowers that never arrived at the house. Her clue into his cheating was his increasingly dangerous behavior of overreacting to life's issues. The stress of cheating, she assumed, was why he threw his glass dinner plate across the room and watched it break into a million pieces on the floor. It's why he punched that hole in the wall and kicked some of the plaster away in another spot in the house. He blamed both incidents on stress at work. The night he almost hit their daughter for the car being out of gas, she wasn't accepting his excuses anymore. When she yelled at him, he apologized and then retorted, "You get to stay at home with the cushy life. I have to go to work each day."

"Maybe he resents me for being a stay-at-home mom," she told me.

"He disrespects you," I said. "You're taking care of four kids and running a house. That is a job."

She found out about the coke, which he said was a habit from the past, as was the booze. The bad moods continued, and I suspect infidelity, too. She hired us, and we uncovered that he still made his drug deals and did coke in the middle of the day in his car. He went back to work and came home raging. Those trips back to work at night? He was really going to local massage parlors and having sex with the girls who worked there. "It's not cheating," he finally confessed. "It's their job to have sex with men."

For his wife, it wasn't a happy ending. She was repulsed by the idea that after his nightly activities, he would come home and have sex with her. "I've never heard of cheating and wanting the wife, too," she said.

We found out that he wasn't just taking creepy to a new level but was also a sex addict who had multiple affairs over the years, plus his massage parlor ladies. A quick trip through his credit card bills revealed trips for two for his mistresses along with flowers and jewelry.

He begged his wife that he would get better. "Could we work it out?" he asked.

The answer was no.

THE MULTIPLE CHEATER

If your spouse has cheated before, you might have made the decision to forgive him or her on the explicit promise that it will never ever ever happen again. The truth is many people follow patterns in their lives. You've heard the phrase "Once a cheater, always a cheater." It's not always true … but it's not always false. There are many who cheat for the thrill of not being caught. They have an affair like Jeremy did on Jenny. All the sneaking around to rundown motels in their town was fun for him and an escape from his otherwise very predictable life as an accountant. There was the adrenaline rush of *almost* being caught, but sliding out of it or coming up with that great excuse that shut down his wife's suspicions until the next time. Yes, there was guilt, but the thrill of knowing he was doing this thing trumped the feeling bad about it. Those types of partners will likely cheat again because they love the thrill of the secret. I would not stay in that kind of relationship, but it's up to each person to set their own limits. Just know that if you're with a thrill seeker, it is likely that their pattern of cheating will continue.

PERFECT LIVES MIGHT NOT BE SO PERFECT

Many of us look at other couples and make false assumptions. We see that handsome, rich man with the beautiful wife and stunning kids and think, *They will be together forever. They have everything. Why would they cheat on one another?* If I only had a dollar for every single time that what looked perfect was not ...

One of my clients was this wonderful, movie-star-handsome man named George, who was wealthy and frankly stunningly good-looking. Even better was that you could feel this aura of authenticity, kindness, and love for his wife and family. They were everything to him. From the outside, one might assume that the wife returned those feelings because the husband was a fine person. He was a very upset one when he called me seven times and could barely say the words, "I think she's cheating on me. If I find out that it's true, I will be utterly destroyed. My family means everything to me."

I knew as a P.I. that he would certainly forgive his wife if she was indeed cheating. And it turned out that she did have a boyfriend on the side to fill her days while the family had her nights. Was she bored? Crazy? Of course, George was devastated because he knew the moment we confirmed with photos that there was some part of his wife's life where she was lacking—and he could not fulfill it. Yes, he blamed himself for her straying. In the end, they did a year of marital counseling, and she promised to never cheat again. To her face, George forgave his wife. He told me privately that it was for the greater family good, and internally he would probably never forgive her. Her excuse for destroying their life? Boredom.

Why someone cheats is often *not* what it seems to the outside world. Most of my clients have wonderful jobs, they're well educated, they have children, and they lead very full lives. Yet, they choose not to be faithful for some reason.

Many times, the rules get bent in the most extreme ways. Years ago, I had a client who confessed a little secret during our first consultation.

"We're swingers," she told me, "but we have rules, too. We cheat in front of each other. But there is a strict rule of no contact with these people before or after the sexual act—and I think my husband is cheating." It turns out that even swingers have their breaking points and this couple got divorced. They agreed to never swing with each other ever again. More rules!

Money doesn't have anything to do with it either. I have a client who owns a $20 million home in Canada and another $15 million lake house. This family is used to the best of the best, including vacations, clothing, and fine wining and dining. The family frequently appears on TV, on red carpets, and in various media outlets. The wife found some odd hotel receipts one day in his desk drawer and confirmed with some snooping into his computer that he was indeed having an affair with one of his PR specialists. There was even a hidden photo file of supposed business trips that doubled as vacations for the two. Did she confront her husband? No.

We confirmed that her husband was indeed cheating with this woman—and it wasn't the first time he had strayed with an employee. Did the wife call a lawyer? No. "I don't like it," she said. "But in the end, I want to continue to be Mrs. Smith and keep my black American Express card and travel to Paris on a whim with my girlfriends. And I want to keep my children's family together."

She asked us to confirm if he was paying for her house and various other bills (yes and yes). And she wanted to know how often they saw each other, which was several times a month. In a safety deposit box in Toronto, there sits an envelope full of the findings of his cheating ways, including photos and videos. She only plans to use it if he asks to leave her someday. She calls it her "damage control."

SHOULD YOU ENGAGE OR RAGE WITH THE OTHER WOMAN OR MAN?

No, no, no, and no. Do not engage. Don't find her phone number and blow your top on the phone. Do not stalk her workplace like Patricia did when she found out that Gina was sleeping with her husband. The last two knew each other from working at the same television station. Patricia was told by other friends at his office that this had been going on (and on) for a long time and included heavy-duty flirting at work. Patricia didn't waste time and went to the TV station, where she quickly threw everything on Gina's desk onto the floor and started screaming at her in front of the entire office.

It's a horrible move because the other party will likely call the police or make an even worse scene. This is not the right way to find any revenge you might be seeking. You might think you have the control over your freak-out, but the second you're standing in front of this person yelling, screaming, and crying, it's you that looks like the nut. Your emotions can't help but take over in the worst way. Yes, you can call her a "whore," but she might say much worse, including that he never loved you. Do not engage with the other party. You only have control of yourself; use it wisely. You will only come off as vindictive with a bruised ego. Remember: Crazy is not good.

Shockingly, it goes both ways. Two people who were married to others had an affair at work. He strayed because his wife was going through breast cancer treatments, and he just couldn't take it. He also promised the woman who was cheating with him that when his wife passed away, he would be free and they would marry after she left her husband. Complicated? My mind was spinning. About six months of sneaking around later, a miracle happened. The wife of the man found out that her cancer was in remission. The same exact day, the phone rang at her house. It was the mistress who decided to put it all on the line. "I've been screwing your husband for the last year," she announced. "He's going to leave you for me."

It was outrageous in so many ways, and that phone call didn't work out well for the mistress. The husband of the cancer survivor was furious, ratted her out to her husband, and then broke it off. Ultimately, both parties divorced, but the two who were cheating never got back together.

Moral of the story: Do not cheat and call or tell. It never works out well for anyone.

KIDS AND INFIDELITY

The saddest cases and the ones that break my heart somehow eventually involve the children of the cheaters. One young man, 10, named Todd, watched as his work-at-home Dad kept going next door in their townhouse development to visit a recently divorced Ginger, the next-door neighbor. One day, Todd decided to sneak through the backyards and look into Ginger's patio door. He found both his dad and Ginger naked in the living room having sex. The kid freaked out, ran home, and called his overbearing grandfather, who raced over to confront his son-in-law. And then Todd's mother, who had no idea anything was going on, came home from work to confront her cheating husband while her own father was in the process of slapping his son-in-law in the face. Todd also witnessed that confrontation, which was a horrible thing for this sensitive child. In the end, there were no winners—especially this traumatized boy.

Those who cheat often become sloppy with their lies. The people who actually catch them with another are often their own kids, who can see right through all the BS. It's heartbreaking, and many adults don't realize that they are causing severe emotional pain, as most children know about divorce and fear it.

I had a client whose wife was the manager of her daughter's youth soccer team. She was having an affair with the coach while her husband was out of town working. Mom also had a good time during weekends away for soccer games and tournaments. Her daughter had a front-row seat to Mom texting the coach, sending sexy pictures, and sneaking off to his room. The kid wasn't stupid. She caught part of all of it, internalized the affair, and began to hate soccer. Her grades began to slip. What most adults don't want to understand is that while you're in the middle of your cheating drama, your own children are like little spies. When Dad grabs flowers on the way home from football practice, but he never gives them to Mom; the kid knows. When Mom "forgets" that there's a sexy message on her iPad that little Timmy borrowed for science homework, the kid is looking and knows. That same child might blurt out over dinner, "Why are you sending my teacher naked pictures, Mommy?" "Where are those flowers you bought for Mummy yesterday?"

In some of the worst-case scenarios, the cheater is destructive enough to bring the child around the person they're cheating with ... insisting that they are just a new friend. The other parent will certainly hit the roof when they find out about the cheating, including that their own child was subjected to this breakage of family trust. Maybe they're even playing house or traveling with the other party.

It's dangerous business because you're playing with your own child's emotional health and future feelings about love, commitment, fidelity, and family.

SAME SEX CHEATING

There are a lot of people who are brought up in certain religions that aren't open to same-sex relationships. They're taught to feel shameful of their true feelings or that they're not acceptable. As these people get older, they realize that they're not sexually or physically attracted to their partner. So, they step outside of their marriage and find happiness in another way. The sad part is their wife/husband often feels really duped and hurt. Some of these cases are quite sad, and others are just one partner cheating on another. Cheating is cheating—no matter if it's with a same-sex partner or the opposite sex.

A client named Sally, a bank executive in New York, came home early one day to her Fifth Avenue condo to find Ted, her husband of ten years, in bed with a man named Mike, who introduced himself as Ted's "long-term boyfriend." Sally was equally shocked when Mike added that he had been longing to meet her because he wanted to know what it would cost to buy her out of the condo—drapes and furniture included.

Several months later, Sally did leave after finding out that Ted never planned on coming out until both of his parents were dead. She had a nice, fat check, the family dogs, and a new house in Florida, where she met a man she knew in high school. They were married two years later and are still in a loving, faithful relationship. And no, she never answered Mike's texts when he inquired about her decorator's phone number.

KICKING THE CHEATER OUT

She cheated. She broke your family's moral compass. He said it was an urge that was quenched. That he would never do it again.

You're not buying any of it and want the cheater out of your house—ASAP. Can you just kick a cheating spouse out? Laws are different everywhere, and it's most helpful to check with a lawyer. Of course, you can ask a cheater to leave, and some will in order to spend more time with their new situation.

If a partner is violent or prone to assault, you can call the police, and most likely they will be told to leave the premises. If you keep a hidden voice-activated recorder in your pocket and have a record of the violence (yelling, screaming, threats), it will certainly help to convince local law enforcement that this isn't a safe situation and someone needs to leave. If you feel like you're in danger or your children are in danger, call 911 immediately.

POST-PANDEMIC FALLOUT

Let's call it. The COVID-19 pandemic meant that the world was literally stuck in the house for almost two years. The Internet, quite literally, was our go-to link to the outside world since you weren't seeing or breathing around anyone in person. Many of us went from well-adjusted to lonely people who turned toward the Internet for some bonding, closeness, or new faces.

As the pandemic ends, my phone is literally blowing up with clients who are wondering if their spouses are emotionally cheating on them with someone from the past who reached out or a new face on Facebook who gave them a thrill as the days seemed to become one long run-on sentence. Remember that cheating isn't always about the penis and vagina—a sexual affair. There are many kinds of infidelity, and pouring out your emotions to a third party is technically cheating in my book.

This might be a good time to have a frank talk with your significant other. If you see someone pop up online who feels wrong, ask them about it before it advances to any next level. If they are flirting with someone new, they are stepping outside your union of trust, and it needs to be confronted and not ignored. I can only imagine that there will be a lot of Internet affairs that become sexual affairs as the world reopens and the CDC allows it.

Be honest with yourself, too. If you're doing something online that feels uncomfortable, it's still cheating. If it's a work person or someone you knew in high school and you're having fantasies about them ... cheating, depending on what you agree upon in your marriage or relationship. Deal with it now before the situation is out of control and your mate is calling a P.I.

Remember, there are 31 flavors of ice cream and about 100 flavors of cheating.

IN THE END

Partners do cheat for a number of reasons, which brings up the question: Should you forgive and stay together? In my experience, I've seen couples survive infidelity, and sometimes their relationship is indeed stronger because it was pushed to the limits. Then again, I have a large percentage of clients who come back six months after the therapy and forgiveness and say, "I should have left him or her a long time ago. I wish I never met them."

In the end, if you have children, then I feel you don't wish away the relationship. If you have some happy memories, maybe you don't wish it away. There were things that were great and some not-so-great, but that's life. But it's not every relationship.

My bottom line is you should never regret staying, and you should never stay if addiction or physical violence is involved. Leave in that moment. Nothing is worth your safety and the mental and physical health of your children.

I look at cheating as you were on a journey with this person, and it has now ended or taken a detour. If it feels overwhelming, then all you need to do is decide what you need to do today for your own safety and sanity.

Will you ever trust again?

People retain us for check-ups in new relationships after they have been cheated on in the past or if they're still with the cheater. A client had her husband followed several times, and nothing was wrong. He wasn't cheating, but she needed that checkup for peace of mind. Once duped, she refused to be fooled again. Once betrayed, now cautious.

If you're going to trust somebody, you have to trust them wholeheartedly, but check-ups can be done discreetly. A little therapy or a reconnection weekend might be the only thing in order.

Remember to always trust your gut; never ignore it.

P.I. Tip: *Many cheaters seek to have an affair with other married people. They don't necessarily want to leave the family unit and are looking for someone on the side who feels the same way. The understanding that they won't implode each other's life is often short-lived, but many try to make it about just sex without emotional availability or any thought of a change of address.*

> ## INFIDELITY CHECKLIST
>
> ☐ Take photos of all the evidence you find.
>
> ☐ Gather as much detail as you can to give to your P.I.
>
> ☐ Make sure to change your password, so any correspondence between you and the P.I. is 100 percent protected. If he/she catches a whiff that you have a P.I., it will be a problem.
>
> ☐ Pay attention to sudden changes in appearance, phone usage, time away from home, and password-protected devices that have been changed.
>
> ☐ Pay attention to Facebook relationships, including secret accounts under other names.
>
> ☐ Do not freeze bank accounts or empty them before speaking with a lawyer. You can certainly take out some of the money for your needs, but that is subjective to your normal behavior. Take half if you suspect the other person is draining your accounts. You can leave that half with your lawyer until a court decides who gets it.
>
> ☐ Consult your lawyer when it comes to all real estate or bigger issues.
>
> *You should trust your partner, but if you feel something is wrong, it probably is. Don't ignore your intuition, gut feeling, or Spidey sense.*

RELATIONSHIPS, DATING AND PRE-MARITAL BLISS (NOT SO MUCH)

It starts so simply. Boy meets girl. Girl likes boy. They plan to ride into the sunset towards his house on that hill … until she finds out that he has a live-in girlfriend, his car was just repossessed, and that beautiful home he has on social media came from a magazine advertisement. He lives in a one-bedroom by the airport. And by the way, she isn't so innocent either. She isn't exactly a doctor but a checkout girl at the local grocery store.

Dating is tricky business, especially in our age of meeting each other on the Internet. A generation ago, there was a chance that someone in your circle knew someone in your date's circle. It was called vouching for someone. But, no more in 2022. The way people meet each other is by signing up for a dating service and then cruising through thousands of potential dates. That system comes with several built-in problems, including the fact that one or both of the parties could easily be lying about what they put on their profile. Or perhaps they're just giving you a written utopian version of who they wished they could be … if it wasn't for those two divorces, they're not mentioning the financial issues that they will certainly explain in more depth after the fifth date. Or was that the fifth of never?

Dating is a minefield now, which is why a lot of women and men do hire a P.I. for a deeper dive after a few dates. My clients in this area don't want to get more involved until they can have a second party, such as a professional P.I., do a background check to make sure that everything is on the up-and-up.

I can hear the objections already. What about love? What about trust? The truth is a background check around the third date is a sound idea because chances are you are not in love but in infatuation. Before you take any next steps, including sexually or introducing children to each other, it doesn't hurt to hire a discreet P.I. Yes, this will upset certain single people who will say that you were supposed to go on blind faith that someone you've met on the Internet or through a blind date is an upstanding citizen. It's true that many of us have a murky area in our pasts. Maybe you declared bankruptcy ten years ago. Or you've been divorced twice. Those are certainly issues to consider and discuss.

But what if the person you've met on the Internet has been accused of abusing children or has been arrested many times or did jail time for a crime?

This reminds me of the young woman who met a handsome man who owned his own construction company. He wined and dined her through several dinners. He even "future" talked to her about all the places they could visit together—and waxed poetic about his love of children and dogs. It sounded perfect—almost a little too perfect. Something was nagging at her when she called a P.I. It turns out that Mr. Construction Company had been arrested three times in the recent past for physically abusing his last girlfriend.

She confronted him on it, and he was hurt that she dared hire a P.I.

"I can't trust you," he said.

"Did you go to jail three times because you hit your last girlfriend?" she demanded.

"Those were misunderstandings," he said. "She was the one who started it."

Maybe he was telling the truth. Maybe not. All she knew was that he was six feet two and over 200 pounds.

"You can lose my number," she told him.

DATING—THE SMART WAY

I'm not knocking Internet sites because it's tough for people to meet in our crazy, hurried society where many singles work, work out, and then go home. It's also true that you don't know much more about that girl you met at the gym vs. the one you've met on a slew of Internet sites.

The truth is you only know so much about a new person, which is basically just what they tell you. That nice guy on the train might be a microbiologist to you. Last week, he was a school principal to that other lovely lady. And then there is that wonderful-sounding woman in your SoulCycle class who says that she is divorced when the truth is she's barely separated and her "husband" is currently sleeping in the basement of their marital house.

Take the case of Ida, who began dating Tommy. Both were professionals who worked for the government. "I'm divorced," she told him, and it made sense. Tommy visited her condo, and the closets were free of any male clothing. The funny thing about Ida is that she was free to date Mondays through Thursdays, but not on the weekends. Tommy decided to follow her and discovered that her family had the condo and then a country home where they all got together on weekends. Ida wasn't divorced; she was simply living closer to her job and cheating on her husband, but only on Mondays through Thursdays.

Here is a checklist of what you should ask a P.I. to look into when it comes to that new person you're "uncovering," which is really a better word for dating.

P.I. Tip: *It's better to be proactive than reactionary in matters of love and romance. That means that it's better to find out who someone really is—historically, emotionally, and financially—before you're ten years and two kids later.*

DATING/PREMARITAL CHECKLIST

☐ Ask for a full background check. There are over 2,000 items that can be checked, but any basic background check will include employment history, financial history, and any criminal activities, including arrest records or proof of jail time served. You will want to know if someone has declared bankruptcy. Have they been married one, two, or ten times? Do they have a career or a job? Any arrests for overusing drugs and alcohol? Also, what do they own? Many people will tell you that the property is their house and they own it when it's really a rental.

☐ Dig up their romantic past. This can be done a number of ways, including seeking out and speaking with past girlfriends or wives. Exes are filled with information, including what happened within their own past relationship. Was there an affair? Abuse? Wives plus mistresses? Women are especially apt to be helpful in ratting out an ex. Yes, some of the info must be taken with a grain of salt. Exes can also be vengeful.

☐ Surveillance. A private investigator can follow your new love interest to see where they go and with whom. This is especially helpful when figuring out if someone is lying about employment within a certain industry. There was a famous case in the U.S. when a man told his new girlfriend that he was an ear, nose, and throat doctor at a big hospital when the truth was he worked at a medical supplies store. A man had his "psychologist" girlfriend followed only to find out that she didn't work at all but spent most days in the park or hanging out at home collecting unemployment. Surveillance is also a good way to see if your new person is dating others ... or perhaps married to someone else.

☐ Track their vehicle. A GPS device can be attached to monitor a love interest's movements. You'll soon find out if their week includes trips to the local massage parlor or strip joint. Or maybe they're attending soccer practice for a child they've failed to mention.

☐ Monitor online activity. Maybe your new love interest is still looking for dates on all of the social sites, or they're in chat rooms for various fetishes. A skilled P.I. can dig deep and uncover suspicious online activity.

☐ Search for property ownership. It's part of the basic background check, but you might want to dig deeper here. Does your new man or woman have a love nest elsewhere? Have they never owned a home?

DO A LITTLE DIGGING

I can't count how many times someone has said to me, "You should be a relationship expert." You can be one, too, if you really listen to what someone else is saying to you. It's tough to meet anyone who has potential, so when you do meet him or her, it's only natural to let a little of the evidence being presented slide by the wayside.

I had a client who was doing a long-distance dating thing with a businessman in California. Early on, he mentioned that his ex was in fact a wonderful friend, and he couldn't wait to introduce the two women. That seemed fine until he brought it up again on the next date and casually let it slide that the ex was living with him. For now. Again, my client let it slide, figuring this wouldn't last forever ... but it did. In fact, they were still living together and had been since their divorce five years ago. This time she had to have "the talk." She was aghast when her new boyfriend said, "Joan and I aren't really divorced, but that's okay because we're not really together."

Pay attention to what someone is telling you—even if it comes out in little drips. You can't ignore the truth, or you're the one who will get hurt in the long run. People will show you and often tell you exactly what they're doing. If you're accepting of odd behavior, I promise that it will probably get stranger as time passes. Red flags are there for a reason, including saying, "This kind of relationship is not for me."

P.I. Tip: *Don't let hindsight kick you in the can. Listen to your gut or intuition and avoid looking back at a disaster in hindsight.*

David was a music manager in his late 40s who just broke up with his twentysomething girlfriend, Heather. A week later, he decided that he would date someone more age-appropriate because he wanted to have a house and a family. He met Cheryl, a PR expert, and immediately smothered her with all of the good stuff. He sent two dozen red roses, arranged dinners at the most expensive restaurants in the city, and used his work relationships to secure fifth-row tickets to the Rolling Stones.

David met Cheryl's family at Thanksgiving, which was three weeks after they met, and love bombed her mother with special desserts, flowers, and candles. Two months into daily talks with Cheryl, something odd happened one night. She called him at their designated time and heard just one click before the answering machine picked up. That meant he was on the phone, which was no big deal. He did business at odd hours. The same thing happened the next night during their regular time. Cheryl planned to talk about it over the weekend, but David said it was no big deal. Neither was the fact that they didn't have sex. He was tired. A cold was coming on. So was Valentine's Day ... and nothing. Not even a card. And she flew in to see him. Dinner was a frozen pizza out of the freezer, and he was too consumed with work to do anything fun that night except fall into bed and start snoring. He cuddled ... the dog.

A few days later, David couldn't be found at all. He didn't return her calls for two weeks until a mutual business issue meant he had to come to the phone.

He was sorry. He got back together with Heather over the holidays. But he wasn't sure, so he didn't want to let Cheryl go. Two months later, he had broken up with Heather again. This meant a quick fling with Kate before going back to Heather again.

David was one of those guys in love with the first flash of being in love. Those are heady, exciting days of showering the new person with fairy tale love, but once it got real, well, he was out. Once it became ham sandwiches by the kitchen sink vs. a five-star dinner, he was bored.

Heather was young and eager to come back. In fact, he finally married her, and two kids later found out that she was cheating on him. "He checked out six months after the wedding," she said.

One of his longest infatuation-ships.

A FEW WAYS TO BE YOUR OWN LOVE P.I.

- File away what he or she is telling you. If she keeps talking about Mark then maybe they're more than friends. You're going to need to find out.
- Meet the family and friends. This might be a scary proposition in a new relationship, but consider this research. You can learn a lot about a person by meeting the inner circle. Be wary of someone who never wants you to meet the friends or family. They could be leading a double life.

P.I. Tip: *If they never bring you around their friends and family, there is a reason.*

- When it's safe, you should see where the person lives, which is also telling. Beware of a house that doesn't feel like a home. If there are no photos of your new man or woman or empty frames, then it's either not their house or they took the married photos away. Remember that it's easy these days to rent an Airbnb and say it's their home. Check out the address on Airbnb. Ask to see a family photo album once you're at the house.
- Of course, you should run from anyone who asks you for money early in a relationship or even later. Val was dating Peter, who was separated and came to her three weeks into their dating relationship hat in hand. He really wanted to get divorced so they could be together but needed her to loan him the money for a lawyer. Val had an inheritance and

could afford it but showed him the door. It wasn't her financial responsibility to pay for his divorce.

P.I. Tip: *If you think you're being taken advantage of ... then you are.*

- Pay attention to drinking and drugs. She pounds down three shots on the first date. He smokes a lot of weed in your backyard on date number two. You should notice your date's relationship with drugs and alcohol, including prescription drugs for a bad shoulder or hurt leg. Ask: What do you take for the pain? How often? Or, do you smoke weed every single day? How often do you go out to the bars? Have your eyes wide open when it comes to these relationship breakers. Even in the early stages of a relationship, you will be able to "see" much more than you think you're seeing.

P.I. Tip: *Don't ignore the red flags out of a fear of being alone or lonely. It's better for your mental health and pocketbook to be alone than with a nightmare partner.*

YOU'RE GETTING MARRIED!

Congratulations! If you are considering saying "I do," I want to implore you to know everything you can about your intended before the big day. You already know I'd like you to hire a P.I. It's imperative that one way or the other you will "beyond a shadow of a doubt" know the following before you walk down that aisle.

- **Criminal history.** Pretend that you're hiring this person … and you are bringing them into the family business of family. A criminal history check is one of the most common background checks. You or your P.I. will look for a record of arrests, convictions, and jail sentences, as well as other public court records.
- **Social media imprint.** Most of us spend a good part of every single day on social media. A background check on your intended will reveal all of his social media links and accounts. Check out their friends lists. What do they talk about on these sites?
- **Identity checks.** Identity fraud is not just a plot device on *Mad Men*. It's a growing problem. You need to look for identity issues on two levels. First, you want to ensure that the person you marry is who they say they are and that they aren't hiding aspects of their life from you. In addition, if he or she has suffered any identity theft issues, you'll want to be informed since this could affect your shared life.
- **Marital status.** Has your new partner been married in the past? Kids? How did this relationship end? It's time to hear the whole story, and perhaps from several parties. True, his ex might tell you some lies, but listen to all of it. It's also key here to make sure that your future spouse is indeed legally divorced from a prior marriage. This will save time, money, and embarrassment when you apply for your own marriage license.
- **Financials.** Marriage is the joining of financial assets and a business when you think about it because you're merging lives and money. You must find out as much as possible about your future mate's financial status. Life insurance? Accounts? Stocks? At least, get a general idea. Properties owned? How much does he or she owe on credit cards? Mark loved Lindsay but found out a month into their

marriage (when the bills were due) that she was over $87,000 in debt with credit cards, while Mark paid his cards off in full each month. This severely impacted their future home purchases. Better to talk about it now vs. later. Yes, this is also the time to protect yourself with a prenup.

All of this focus on finding out and money might sound unromantic, but breaking up and divorce don't involve Cupid either. If you do your due diligence at the beginning of a relationship, you will save yourself mental grief and money. So, what if your partner feels as if you're invading his or her privacy? They should want you to have peace of mind. And if there is nothing to hide, then what is the problem?

People who are nice, kind, and lovable often get duped when in love. I've never had someone call me five years later and say, "I wish you didn't find out that Steven had those two wives that he didn't divorce because I would have rather it remained a surprise." You want to know so you can move on and find love interests who aren't perfect but are on the same moral course as you throughout life.

QUESTIONABLE BEHAVIOR

It's amazing how many lunatics are out there masquerading as normal people. All day long and into the wee hours of the morning, my phone rings with announcements of what one might call textbook or regular bad behavior, including that he's cheating or she's cheating or they're stealing money from the joint bank account. Those are the by-the-book cases, and I know what to say: "First and foremost, consult your lawyer. Keep everything hush-hush; start a collection of bank statements or a financial snapshot of the last two years. I'll tell the client to take some of the money and a little bit more to live on or to pay the legal fees. Again, your lawyer can talk to you about leaving the premises unless you're in danger, and then call 911 and leave now. Your attorney will talk to you about freezing assets or clearing out an account.

Those are the so-called normal calls. Then again, everyone seems normal until they're not.

In other words, the world is an ever-changing place, and it's hard to just trust situations as they seem because it might be a case of what I call questionable behavior. You might call it "odd behavior," but there is an ongoing shift in these post-pandemic times in what actually constitutes odd or normal.

Many people's lives were teetering before the pandemic. Perhaps stress or living on the edge constituted a life where odd things to some became normal to them. Maybe they're even living some kind of a secret life, and their partner has absolutely no idea. As long as they're only potentially hurting themselves, they reason, it's okay to have a secret life.

I call this questionable behavior.

Questionable behavior could be everything from infidelity with a friend or family member to strange online relationships to a sex addiction or an eating disorder that's kept quiet. It could be habits like secretly going to strip or massage parlors. Maybe it's a well-hidden drinking or drug habit or other substance abuse due to a midlife crisis. They pay to have a girlfriend or boyfriend stashed in an apartment. They have a thing for … things that are outside society's laws or moral rules, including certain types of porn.

Questionable behavior often results in a life filled with deception and lies of various magnitudes. Take the 40-ish overweight woman who is diabetic but sneaks to three different ice cream parlors each day to binge eat or the man who buys and buys and buys things he doesn't need online because of a shopping addiction. People often lose jobs and marriages due to their questionable behavior habits, which are often the result of lingering mental health issues.

Therapy can help, as can full disclosure to a loving spouse committed to help even if it's a long journey.

One thing is certain: Questionable behavior can ruin your life and gut your family.

DISCOVERING QUESTIONABLE BEHAVIOR: A CASE STUDY

Charlotte and Jim have been married for ten years. They met at their mutual accounting office, dated for a year, and then got hitched. Three kids later, she is a busy working mom who volunteers at school, while Jim is a workaholic and coaches his son's softball team on the weekends. Jim takes his wife out for a nice Saturday night dinner and attends church with the family on Sundays. From all accounts, it's a busy, stressful, and pretty normal family life.

Except …

Once a month, Jim goes on a work trip to visit clients in a nearby city. Charlotte didn't think twice about these trips. He called her when he was leaving; he called her before he went to bed. He told her about the weather and the bad out-of-town chicken dinners. She was never suspicious of these trips until she saw something on television about checking your husband's or wife's credit card statement. Why this nagged at her … she had no idea. But she knew Jim's password to his business, or at least she thought she knew it. It took her five tries to get it right.

She found his hotel receipts and took a little jog down the list of expenses to find that Jim had an odd charge during each business trip. It was $200 charged to the pool at the little boutique hotel he frequented. The other charges were in black, but the pool charge was always in green and not a part of the total bill, as Jim covered it with his own funds before leaving. He never listed the pool charges on his expense reports.

She figured it was a mistake. Her husband wasn't one to even sit by a pool, plus they lived in a cold-weather climate. What the heck was he doing at a pool in the middle of winter?

Calls to the hotel didn't help until finally she called the concierge and pretended that her boss had an upcoming trip to the hotel. She inquired about pool charges. She was asked: brunette or blonde? It turns out pool charges were code for hooker charges at this hotel.

Mild-manner Jim had a thing for hookers and ordered them to his room for years. He made sure to pay for this part of his trip in cash on the way out, so his bosses didn't question the charge. A few times, one slipped through, and he blamed it on a massage for his bad back.

Charlotte was shocked. They had what she thought was a good enough sex life.

When she hired a P.I., Charlotte found that Jim had a lifelong pattern of sneaking around, hiring hookers, and visiting strip clubs and massage parlors when he was out of town. The P.I. shot photos of Jim checking into the hotel and then meeting women in long coats in the lobby. In fact, he usually padded each business trip with an extra day so he could enjoy himself.

Jim was shocked and embarrassed when confronted but admitted that he couldn't stop. He didn't even want to stop despite his wife's health concerns.

She began divorce proceedings immediately but stopped short of ratting out her husband at work. His job funded their entire family, and her P.I. assured her that she didn't need financial issues, too. Oh, and Jim went along with all of her requests because to this day, he still frequents the pool when he's on the road.

Background Checks: The New Relationship Tool

It would be nice to trust people, but the truth is you can unfortunately uncover a lot of questionable behavior during a standard background check. People might think that they're being highly secretive with their odd behaviors, but most aren't so tricky and leave the clues that are there to be found. If you look for them.

We live in an age of cameras everywhere, with documentation just a few clicks away on the Internet. It's easy for people to begin their own investigations by jumping on the computer.

However, if you think it might be a case of questionable behavior,

I'd advise you to give this case to a professional P.I. During these murky cases, it becomes increasingly obvious that those who engage in questionable behavior deal with other fringe types of people who might be dangerous. The last thing most of us need is to purposely thrust ourselves into a dangerous situation, which is why I like to go with the pros. The detective I assign knows how to navigate some of the rougher areas of town, unlike an emotionally distraught wife looking for clues in a part of the city that is guaranteed to be dangerous.

P.I. Tip: *You can put your head in the sand when it comes to questionable behavior. Me? I'd want to know. You don't want a life filled with bad surprises.*

OTHER FAMILIES

Teri is a 42-year-old writer who met Bill at a charity event. They spent the following year engaged in a beautiful long-distance love affair of meeting up somewhere charming and upscale twice a month for a weekend together. Bill, who barely talked about a marriage that didn't work with his college sweetheart, eagerly listened to Teri's multi-decade dating horror stories. She didn't push to meet family and friends; neither did he. About eight months into the relationship, he invited her to his house for one of their weekends. It was odd in that there were children's toys and a swing set in the yard. He assured her that his sister, who had just divorced, was living with him for a little while. She was eager to believe it—except for the female clothing in the master bedroom closet.

Bill had an answer for that one. He always had some kind of reason why. "I barely have any closet space in the house, and my sister doesn't want her teenage daughter stealing clothes," he said, reassuring her that it wasn't "anything weird. My sister sleeps on the couch in the den."

Time passed, and Teri began to really notice Bill's behavior, including how he talked on his cell in the bathroom or was constantly texting someone he claimed was work. It was on a second weekend visit to Bill's house that she decided to dig a bit deeper. A kitchen desk drawer revealed that the household bills were in the name of Bill and Anne.

"Is your sister also on the electric bill?" Teri demanded in her most snide tone.

Yes, Bill was married. With children. His youngest daughter was a gymnast, so when his wife and kids left town for a weekend retreat, he lived on the edge. What was more exciting than tempting fate by bringing his new girlfriend home. Imagine how Bill had to rush to clean the house and change the sheets after dropping Teri off at the airport and before his family came home.

Bill's questionable behavior included the idea that he was constantly talking about his future with Teri when they were together. They even had a timetable to get engaged the following spring.

Sadly, this couple is not alone. There are many men and women who are married, yet they live double lives. Some even marry two partners and live off the adrenaline of trying to "be there" for both families. Those who do this are often narcissists who only care about what they want and don't care about how their bad behavior will hurt everyone involved. This is almost worse than having an affair because having a secret family is declaring that you're in love with someone else and what's going on in just one home will never be enough.

Some of these situations even begin as a secret affair and end up as two families that must be supported. The man or woman with the questionable behavior will often claim to truly love the original family.

Tess had an affair with a married man and became pregnant with his child. She couldn't admit to what she had done, so she passed her new son off as her original husband's baby. She even lied to the man she was having the affair with and agreed to marry him. After they eloped, she split her time, insisting that the rest of the time was spent out of town for business. It was an epic mess that involved sneaking around making calls or secret texts. Eventually both men found out, and she found herself alone.

Why don't these people just divorce and remarry? Many times, they don't want the judgment from their families, or they fear having to give away half of their savings. In the end, there is often more pain, more expense, and small children who are in the middle of these heinous situations. Don't listen to excuses about loving two different people. Our society mandates that you marry just one. When you have two families, you're simply cheating on everyone.

HOW DOES SOMEONE FIND OUT ABOUT A SECOND FAMILY?

Here are a few at-home P.I. tips on how to figure this out:

- **Tax returns.** Even if you're not the person doing the tax returns, it's your right to look at the finished work before it's turned in to the government. Pay attention to how many dependents your spouse lists.
- **Someone with your same last name.** If your surname is unusual, then pay attention when it's called at a restaurant or airport. Of course, there are many with the same last name, but if you have a nagging feeling, then introduce yourself or start a conversation.
- **Eyewitness reports.** You're running around town and decide to take a break at a local park. There's your dad, which is odd for a Wednesday night. He's actually hugging a little girl and walking hand-in-hand with a strange woman.
- **Mom or Dad meeting a cousin.** You see a strange child or older person in a mall who hugs your mother or father. You've never seen this person before in your life. Mom or

Dad passes the stranger off as a cousin. But the talking portion that follows is much more immediate and personal. It's funny how a "cousin" can become a secret daughter

- **A confession.** You're at work, and a stranger shows up saying she's your father's other wife or Mom's other husband. It's all right there on the table for further discovery.
- **DNA tests.** These DNA tests that require you to spit into a tube and then send results have produced many family reunions.
- **Weird coincidences.** Two high school seniors looked enough alike to question it, plus they had the same middle and last names.
- **The funeral.** You can't make this up. There are many cases when two different families show up at the same funeral. Imagine the shock when children, who don't know each other, arrive to bury Dad, and two wives are shocked to meet for the first time.

P.I. Tip: *Go into relationships with your eyes wide open—and keep them open. If you ignore it, that doesn't mean it will go away. No, it's not romantic to dig into what your spouse is really doing, but it's smart. Knowledge is power.*

CASE STUDY: THE TICKLE TRUNK

A wife hired us because she suspected that her otherwise loving husband, who doted on her and their three kids, was having some kind of midlife crisis. We dug deeper, and she said that they had a wonderful sex life and otherwise solid relationship. She was even cool when it came to the idea that he liked to get a little kinky in bed, although that was dying down. He didn't seem happy about much anymore, which concerned her.

Our P.I.'s followed him around and unearthed the fact that her hubby was meeting different females each day at high-end restaurants. By the looks of these meetings, it was almost as if they were job interviews. The girls were very nervous and very young. Back at his car, he would always leave his trunk open. Our P.I.'s spotted the one thing that he had in there: a safe.

I prayed that there wasn't a gun in there, but that was a possibility because the man would open the safe and grab a duffle bag from inside it that could be hiding something like a firearm. I was about to alert the authorities when the wife broke into it. There were his toys: strap on dildos, various other sex toys, a ton of feathers, wads of cash, gags, blindfolds and other item he could enjoy with these youthful escorts that he hired for some lively afternoons.

OTHER FORMS OF QUESTIONABLE BEHAVIOR

Sex Addiction

A big part of the thrill here is the idea of getting caught. Take Adam, who had a gorgeous wife who was happy to have sex with him every single day, but it wasn't enough. She was an apple, and he didn't want apples all the time. He loved the temptation of other women, which he equated to being his drug of choice.

Instead of having long-term affairs, Adam frequented local strip clubs and massage parlors. He cruised Craigslist,where everything is sold from sex to vacuum cleaners. Adam wasn't just addicted to the sex but also to the thrill of being bad. He really loved his wife, but he got itchy for the kind of excitement a new sexual partner brought to his life.

The shock here is his wife found out and decided to accept it. "Listen," she said, "I'm raising three kids. The truth is I'm not a highly sexual person. I'd rather him do it with strangers than screw our nanny or have a secret relationship with one of my girlfriends."

Adam was allowed to scratch his itch. "I'm a human being. I'm a man. I need this," he said.

Adam, it turns out, was also a sex addict. He was not just risking his family life, but his health (and the health of his wife) by engaging in risky sexual behavior.

Clues: Some early signs include spending time with online porn and online relationships. This morphs into going to strip clubs and hiring escorts or hookers. Many times, this isn't a choice but an actual addiction that will require therapy. Other clues include password changes, enormous amounts of time at the computer, often late at night, disappearing, and changes in sex habits at home. Yes, this is infidelity and can also expose the other partner to a myriad of diseases.

Help: Therapy is key, as promises to "just stop" are often short-lived.

Gambling Addiction

A suburban mom and lawyer recently had to confess to her husband that she lost over $100,000 over the last month from playing poker on a local gambling boat. This wasn't the first time that a big chunk of the family savings was secretly handed over to a dealer because she has a gambling addiction—and has had one since college. Her wagers over football were too big, and her trips to Vegas left her "in the hole" for months. These days this type of questionable behavior includes gambling bitcoin.

Clues: Bank accounts are cleaned out, life savings are lost, and college funds are drained because one partner cannot stop gambling. They're always out of the house. A local gambling place becomes a regular Friday or Saturday night hangout. The dealers at the ultra-expensive table seem to know your wife/husband by heart. Wins are not good enough. Partner is constantly stressed about money. Partners lose life savings or even their jobs to go sit in a car or library day trading. The thrill of gambling cannot be matched. Even small bets like $5 with your child over some mundane issue become the norm.

Help: Family therapy and a financial advisor working hand-in-hand can fix the crisis. The other partner can also list the gambling addict's name at various gambling ships as someone who is not allowed in.

Substance Abuse

Weed. Coke. Pills. Booze. No one starts out wanting to become an alcoholic or drug addict. They go down a road like Carol did, where a few glasses of wine at lunch with girlfriends becomes an entire bottle by herself and a DUI conviction and divorce. Drugs and alcohol take most people outside of their daily life and give them the false courage to deal with things. They drown their sorrows or toke up to chill out. It often starts in their 20s in college, but it's not the same thing at 40.

Clues: Time that can't be accounted for during the day or night, plus frequent trips to the liquor store. There are also unexplained expenses and time spent "sleeping it off." It's also tough to hide the smell of pot or booze. In the worst cases, people drink and get high or drunk, and this becomes a police issue with an expensive DUI involving bodily harm or manslaughter.

Help: The time to stop is now. I've watched drugs and alcohol hurt so many families. Help your partner stop it now before they kill themselves or others. An intervention with family and friends can even help you drive your mate towards a stint at a local rehab center.

Food Addiction

It might start off as no big deal. When your wife is feeling emotional, she overeats at dinner or jumps into a big bag of chocolate chip cookies. In other cases, she doesn't want to have sex with her husband as much, so a weight issue becomes an obesity one. Just like alcohol, people eat too much food to self-soothe. Joyce was unhappy in her marriage, so she overate at meals, which morphed into a daily trip to the grocery where she would sit in the parking lot and eat two pints of ice cream. She hides candy bars in the bathroom. A few times, she has tried sticking her fingers down her throat to throw up, which could easily lead to an eating disorder. Such behavior isn't just a woman's issue. Men often go through bags and bags of chips and orders of pizza on weekends in the name of watching football. In all cases, the pounds are piling up, and the family doctor is warning that type 2 diabetes is next.

Clues. Some of them include significant weight gain or loss. The person often doesn't eat with the family, or they eat like a mouse, although they are quite overweight. You might see them smuggling cookies or an extra hamburger to eat later in their office or bedroom. Household money is missing, and grocery bills are soaring. Credit card bills reflect too many restaurant visits.

We had a case where the wife thought he was having an affair. Each night, her husband insisted on going for a walk alone. She begged him to walk together, but he needed that time alone. She also noticed money was missing. One night, she followed him and watched as he hit up three fast food places after having a full dinner. This was why he wasn't losing weight. He was eating tacos and burgers and fries as an after-dinner treat. They went to therapy, and it turned out that he had been sexually abused as a younger child and food was his one trusted friend. Once he worked through his issues, he began to lose weight.

Help: Family or personal therapy along with the hiring of a nutritionist often helps in the treatment of a food addiction. Exercise that is fun is also a way to reduce stress and keep the overeating to a minimum.

Mental Health Issues

One of the biggest areas of questionable behavior revolves around mental health issues. It always begins the same way for our agency. The phone will ring and the voice at the other end will say, "I know you're going to think I'm crazy, but …"

I've had calls, including from the woman who insisted the government was spraying blue mist into the vents of her house. "They came in and put a chip in my brain," she cried. Another man was sure his wife was cheating on him. How did he know? "My toilet seat told me," he said.

I don't hang up the phone right away. I will speak to the person and ask if they have anyone at home or a phone call away who can talk about their fear. Often, I will hear, "Yes, I have my wife … and she thinks I'm crazy." Many of these people want to hire me. I'll ask to speak to their wife or husband or child and often hear sad stories that indicate their family member is dealing with mental issues. The thing to remember is that this person is utterly convinced that these strange things are really happening.

Last week, a man called me because he was convinced that aliens had landed on his front lawn. "You don't know. There are so many government things that are hidden," he said. It was a bit sad because this man clearly needed some type of help. I spoke with the man's wife, who told me, "Honey, I've seen the aliens, too." They both needed help because there wasn't the mental capacity there to make other life decisions.

All I can do in these cases is offer a support line. I also realize that people are terrified these days in our post-COVID world. They're dealing with anxiety, grief, and loss and living in an extremely anxious way. There is depression and PTSD, so I'd like to advise everyone to be kind in these situations and not make fun of or argue with those who are suffering.

Remember, too, that people are lonely after two years in lock-up. Sometimes telling a so-called crazy story is their way to get a little attention. If this is out of control, you can always contact social services in your town or the police if you feel any true danger is there.

Clues: Those with mental health issues often talk about stuff that isn't true. Their realistic cognitive behavior seems off. Maybe this is a relative or elderly neighbor who is acting very different or has paranoid, unrealistic visions. If this is you, perhaps you're not sleeping anymore or questioning why no one seems to believe you anymore.

Help: Reach out to local social services or the police. You can also contact your family doctor, who can administer tests.

Shopping Addiction

My favorite addiction, and hopefully my husband doesn't hire a P.I. on me, is a shopping addiction. It's true that women seem to shop more than men, although I know some guys who can burn up a credit card. We call it retail therapy. If it's not outrageous, you can pass it off as an indulgence. But there are some people who have actual shopping addictions. They overspend and then spend some more without even thinking about paying the bills. They put their families at risk financially because they can't stop.

A man called me because he was sure that his wife was having an affair. She had just started a new job, lost twenty pounds, and was acting differently. She got blowouts for her hair, and her nails were always "done" now. She checked all the boxes for an affair, but we ended up following her only to find out she was having an affair with her credit cards. She was a shopping addict who actually rerouted all the credit card bills to go paperless. Her new password kept her husband out of her online accounts. One day, the phone rang at home from a shop she loved, and they messed up by calling her. "Your Louis Vuitton has arrived," the salesgirl said. "Your Alexander McQueen is also here." The bad news was the family was now $180,000 in debt.

Clues: Your mate is dressing differently. Bags keep showing up on your front step. Open his or her closet, and all you see is a bunch of tags. Credit card statements are rerouted, so there isn't a paper trail anymore. When you go into a store with your spouse, everyone knows her by name. They know your kids by their first names. Funds have gone missing, and credit card balances are sky-high. Your credit score takes a dive because he/she missed payments.

Help: Call your local therapist and accountant. Limit credit cards to one with a limit. Temporarily suspend use of mutual bank accounts.

Strength isn't something you find after the storm—it's something you sharpen in the middle of it. You don't need a perfect plan, a clean history, or anyone's permission to take control of your life. What you need is what you already have: the ability to read between the lines, to trust your gut when something doesn't sit right, and to move with conviction when the stakes are high. Every red flag, every hard truth, every moment that demanded more than you thought you had—it all built you. And now, you know too much to go back to who you were before. You're not here to play it safe. You're here to move smarter, stand taller, and choose yourself with unwavering clarity. That's power. That's leadership. That's how you rise.

THANK YOU FOR RISING WITH US

You didn't just turn the page—you turned a corner in your story. *Rockstar Rising* is more than a book. It's a declaration that your voice matters, your vision is beautiful, and your journey is powerful. Welcome to a global sisterhood that sees you, believes in you, and stands beside you as you rise. You're not alone. You're in the front row now—and we're just getting started.

I Am Unbreakable is not just a brand—it's a global movement for women who lead, build, and break the mold.

Founded by international speaker and resilience expert Adrianne Fekete, I Am Unbreakable stands at the intersection of leadership, entrepreneurship, Rockstar-level confidence, and resilience. Our work reaches over 250,000 women worldwide who are tired of playing small and ready to claim the spotlight they were born for. My vision is to drive social impact, document legacies, and foster the belonging of a billion women globally.

"Women don't need permission to build empires—just a platform to be seen building them."

We are the *go-to platform* for trailblazing women and the Support-HERs who champion them. Through our award-winning magazine, unapologetically unfiltered podcast, live experiential events, and front-row sister community, Where Bold Women Rise, and Legends Are Made

I Am Unbreakable® Magazine
The official magazine of bold disruptors, changemakers, and next-level leaders. We feature real stories from women who are building empires, rewriting rules, and redefining what success looks like—on their own terms.

The I Am Unbreakable® Podcast
Unfiltered, unshakeable, and wildly human. Hosted by Adrianne Fekete and Chris McMartin, each episode is a front-row seat to the lessons, pivots, power plays, and unbreakable truths of fierce founders and women who refuse to stay quiet.

Live Experiential Events That Transform Lives
From The Power of the Pitch to the I Am Unbreakable® Summit to Rockstar Master Classes, our high-voltage events are where bold visions meet real momentum. Women founders take the stage to share their journey, inspire others, build powerhouse connections, elevate innovation, and pitch for capital. They leave armed with strategy, a new front-row sister community, wings, and unshakable confidence.

Front Row Sisters Community
If you're here, you're not just interested—you're ready.
Ready to lead bolder.
Ready to turn resilience into your superpower.
Ready to join the women rewriting what's possible.

Thank you for rising with us.
Thank you for showing up—for yourself and for every woman who needs to see what's possible. Thank you for stepping into something bigger than you.

By holding this book, you've said yes to growth, grit, and greatness. *Rockstar Rising* is a movement. A reminder that your strength isn't up for debate, and your story doesn't need polishing to be powerful. We see you. We back you. And we're building a world where women rise bolder, lead stronger, and never question if they belong. Because you do. This is your front row. This is your movement. And we're honored to have you in it.

ROCKSTAR CONFIDENCE ACTION CHECKLIST

Use this page to track your growth by reviewing each chapter's key action step. Come back to this list anytime you need a reset or a reminder of who you are becoming.

- ☐ **Rockstar Confidence.** Record a voice memo of three affirmations. Play it every morning for seven days.
- ☐ **The Resilience Revolution.** Write a letter to your younger self thanking them for surviving.
- ☐ **Rejection is Redirection.** Make a timeline of redirections that became blessings.
- ☐ **Manifest Like a Rockstar.** Write your vision in the present tense and post it visibly for thirty days.
- ☐ **The Three F-Bombs.** Take one brave step toward something fear has kept you from.
- ☐ **Own Your Shift.** Declare your next shift out loud. Share it with someone who'll support you.
- ☐ **Nice Gut.** Keep a seven-day journal tracking intuitive hits and gut feelings.
- ☐ **Comfortable Being Uncomfortable.** Do something that stretches your comfort zone.
- ☐ **Perfectly Imperfect.** Say three affirmations out loud in the mirror.
- ☐ **From Trauma to Purpose.** Reach out to someone grieving and offer your presence.
- ☐ **The Power of I Am.** Say five new "I Am" statements out loud each morning this week.
- ☐ **You Are A Rockstar.** Write your Unbreakable Manifesto: who you are, what you stand for, and what comes next.

This is your backstage pass to resilience, grit, and unapologetic self-leadership. You're here to choose yourself and boldly own it. Let's rise so you can be the Rockstar you were born to be!

THANK YOU FOR READING MY BOOK!

Welcome to Your Rise; This Is the Beginning of Everything

The struggle is part of the story. And so is your comeback. Whether you whispered "enough" or screamed "I'm ready," something brought you here—and that something matters.

Rockstar Rising is more than a collection of chapters. It's a mirror, a mission, and a movement. It's proof that your past doesn't define you—your decision to rise does.

Your Comeback Starts Here!

I created a space where bold women rise and legends are made. But it is not just a brand—it's a global movement for those who lead, build, and break the mold.

But rising isn't meant to be done alone. That's why I built the I Am Unbreakable® with our Front Row Sisterhood community in the forefront—a place where the boldest, fiercest, most resilient women gather to support, strategize, and soar. Not someday—now.

This is the moment everything changes.
The front row is waiting for you.

No More Sidelines. No More Silence. Just You, Rising.

Scan the QR code to step into the room built for women who are done waiting. You're not behind. You're right on time.

**YOU DIDN'T JUST PICK UP A BOOK.
YOU ANSWERED A CALL.**

Scan the QR Code Here:

I appreciate your interest in my book and value your feedback, as it helps me improve future versions. I would appreciate it if you could leave your invaluable review on Amazon.com with your feedback. Thank you!

www.ingramcontent.com/pod-product-compliance
Lightning Source LLC
Chambersburg PA
CBHW030242010526
44107CB00030B/1310/J